Habits *for* Holiness

SMALL STEPS FOR MAKING
BIG SPIRITUAL PROGRESS

FR. MARK-MARY AMES, CFR

ASCENSION
West Chester, Pennsylvania

Nihil obstat: Rev. Paschal Maria Coby, CFR
February 4, 2021

Imprimi potest: Rev. John Paul Ouellette, CFR
General Servant
February 4, 2021

Scripture passages are from the Revised Standard Version–Second Catholic Edition, copyright © 2006 Division of Christian Education of the National Council of the Churches of Christ in the United States of America. Used by permission. All rights reserved.

Ascension
PO Box 1990
West Chester, PA 19380
1-800-376-0520
ascensionpress.com

Cover design by Rosemary Strohm

Cover photo by Jeffrey Bruno

Printed in the United States of America
21 22 23 24 25 7 6 5 4 3
ISBN 978-1-950784-60-8

CONTENTS

As you begin to journey with the Lord through this book, may the example of St. Francis inspire you and the prayers of St. Francis sustain you.

Prayer to St. Francis

O St. Francis, stigmatized … [at] La Verna, the world yearns for you as an icon of Jesus Crucified. It needs your heart open towards God and man, your bare and wounded feet, your pierced and imploring hands. It longs for your weak voice, but strong with the power of the Gospel.[1]

—St. John Paul II

Help us! You who brought Christ close to your age, help us to bring Christ close to our age, to our difficult and critical times. Amen.

INTRODUCTION

"Fort Apache" was the nickname given by some to a police precinct in the South Bronx around the 1970s. It was situated in a neighborhood that had all the characteristics of a war zone. There were boarded-up buildings, burned-out cars, regular gunshots echoing up and down the block, frequent violence, and deaths by shootings, drug overdoses, and knife wounds. Gangs were doing their best to run the streets. It really was a war zone.

And in the year 1987, when God in his providential wisdom and timing decided to inspire a new Franciscan reform, he chose to plant this new Franciscan seed in the shade of the so-called Fort Apache precinct in the South Bronx. From the outside looking in, it seemed like a neighborhood of chaos in the most infertile of soils. But it was here—precisely and providentially here—that the Holy Spirit began what would become the Franciscan Friars of the Renewal. Under the care of the archbishop of New York, John Cardinal O'Connor, friars moved into St. Crispin Friary in the South Bronx. And as they could still hear yelling and violence on the streets—as they could hear the destruction left through the wickedness of sin and corruption—the brothers began to pray and do penance. They lived, worshipped, and served together. Their prayer life and their fraternal life overflowed into their apostolic life as they got to know their neighbors and listened to them, loved them, and served them.

As time went on, this little Franciscan seed would develop into a full-grown Franciscan order, an order that received its pontifical status in the year 2016. It was here in the South Bronx, with all its dangers and destruction, that the Holy Spirit inspired and equipped these men to live a life of holiness. Through this holy life, the community and its members were not conformed to the chaos of the neighborhood but became instruments of transformation in hearts and lives, starting with their own. Christianity has a beautiful patrimony. Throughout history, its members enter into chaos and participate in God's work of renewal, rebuilding, reforming, and transforming from within. We've been doing it successfully for centuries, but it doesn't happen by accident.

Light in the Darkness

I begin by sharing the example of the South Bronx and its difficulties and struggles, particularly in the late '80s when the friars moved there, for a reason. I begin with that example because for many people, Fort Apache feels like an appropriate name for every home in the midst of a really dangerous, broken, struggling, and suffering culture. And I personally have many doubts and questions about whether or not I can live a life of holiness amid such disorder and darkness. We often hold even more heartfelt fear for our loved ones, especially our children. We may wonder if it is possible for them to grow up in this world knowing and loving Jesus and following faithfully in his footsteps. Is it possible in this world to live a life of holiness? The answer is yes, it *is* possible, because the light has shone in the darkness, and the darkness has never and will never overcome it (see John 1:5).

From the early centuries of Christianity, Christians have been sent out to be salt and light and leaven in the world, not to be conformed to the world but to transform the world from within. In the early centuries, this took place not only in a spiritual way but also in a natural way. For instance, we have a great tradition of monasteries being set up in swamps and in the most infertile of soils. Amid the monks' time of prayer and communal life and labor, the physical ground was transformed into a flourishing and fertile land. As these monks worked the land spiritually, they also transformed their societies by being pillars of truth, hospitality, stability, and guidance. They shone like bright stars in what must often have felt like a dark world.

Historically, we look to the thirteenth century as a pivotal, transformative moment in the way Christians radically gave their lives to the Lord. No longer were they fleeing to do battle in the desert or stepping outside of the community to build monasteries. Instead, a new expression of religious life started to blossom, in which the whole world would become a cloister. Most notably, the Dominicans, the Carmelites, and the Franciscans began to give examples for living holiness from within the world. These orders, called mendicant orders, can be thought of as "monks on the move." Like other monks, they lived lives totally consecrated to God, but unlike them, they often traveled from town to town preaching the gospel. As had been happening with monasteries and monks for centuries, the laity would flock to these mendicants for guidance and support. And so began a flourishing Franciscan Third Order, which allowed the laity to live Franciscan spirituality formally in a way that was consistent with their state in life. The Franciscans would guide, encourage, inspire, and support the laity in their own journey. And for centuries, the Third Order model was a source of encouragement and guidance for those seeking to live radical discipleship and Catholicism.

Today, there remains this desire in many people to follow Jesus radically. How can I give my life totally to Jesus? And how can I live a life of holiness, especially in a culture and time that is ill but also most in need of the medicine and the healing touch of Jesus and his Church? We look around for models of radical Catholicism and often don't find what we are looking for. They just don't stand out. It's true, certain individuals inspire us, and we look to them as models and mentors. And we have our saints. But I would like to propose going back to the sources somewhat. As a priest of the Franciscan Friars of the Renewal, I'd like to propose the mendicant life—or more particularly, our own Franciscan life—as a model to learn from, adjust where necessary, and apply as a pattern for radically following Jesus today.

We realize that many people do not have the option of fleeing their community to escape the dangers and difficulties of the current society, political structure, and cultural climate. But that's OK. As the Franciscan friars have known through the grace of the Holy Spirit—as they began to do in 1987 in the South Bronx and continue to do today—and as Christians have done for centuries, we are fully equipped and capable of holiness in darkness.

Poco a Poco, Little by Little

In this book, we will take a look at some principles—some pillars—of our Franciscan life. We'll look at prayer, community, liturgical living, simplicity, mission, and our baptismal call. We'll unpack them and then propose them in a way that you can receive and apply to your journey, no matter at what stage in life you find yourself. Taken from the wisdom of the mendicant life (which has existed for eight centuries), these pillars will provide us with a model to follow for living radical discipleship in the world. They will provide strategy and application. What I'd like to propose to you, the reader, is to read this book and then apply it to your life following the *poco a poco* model, "little by little."

We understand that life is a pilgrimage and that our spiritual life, like a physical journey, is made step by step. We're always trying to make the next best step. This book is going to propose an ideal, and a very high ideal, but I don't want you to be discouraged by it if you don't feel like you can achieve it tomorrow. I propose the ideal as a destination, a place to which we're journeying, understanding that a journey may be necessary. As you read, I'm going to ask you to prayerfully invite the Lord to reveal to you what is the next best step. The next best step may be a baby step. The next best step may be a prayer. Or it might be stepping out of the boat as you hear Jesus inviting you to walk on water. But let's continue to make this pilgrimage *poco a poco*, little by little, step by step, always beginning by inviting the Lord to guide us and to help us on the journey.

And I'd like what I propose in this book to be applied *poco a poco*, little by little, strategically and prudently in your own families or communities. Just remember that the next best step for others may not be the same as the next best step for you, so we want to be very prudent and patient about how we bring about cultural changes in our families. We want to be especially prudent if the changes are significant ones where spouses and children are involved. As you read the book, I'm going to ask you to prayerfully consider going wherever you feel the Lord is inviting you, but also talk with and listen to those who are going to be affected by the changes you make. Change can be very difficult, especially when others are involved. But if you apply what you learn in this book prudently, appropriately, and with the guidance of the Holy Spirit, it may bring about even deeper communion among family, community, and the Lord.

From Abstract Concepts to Practical Proposals

If you ask pretty much any adult what it takes to be healthy physically, he or she will respond, "You have to exercise and you have to eat right." It's pretty clear and pretty basic. But often people are not able to lose weight or improve their health. It's not because they don't know what to do but because they only know what to do in an abstract way. Going from the abstract to the practical, though it may feel like a small step, is often a deal breaker. So there's a flourishing business of physical trainers offering workout plans and diet plans. These trainers often propose workouts or meals very specifically, understanding that specifics are helpful for us. Clarity is helpful. At the same time, though, trainers understand that each person is unique, and sometimes their proposals need to be nuanced and adjusted for the individual.

I'm going to take the same model or mindset in this book. Many of you know what it takes to grow in holiness on an abstract level. We'll break down some of these things in a way that is helpful and concrete. But I'm going to go one step even further and offer very practical and specific proposals for the ways you can apply these principles in your life. And I offer them because I think the clarity is helpful; it saves you from taking that extra step of trying to figure it out. At the same time, I offer them with the understanding that these proposals may not be for everyone. So I encourage you to consider them, apply them to your life where possible, nuance and adjust them where necessary, and pass on them when that's appropriate. I'm going to throw a lot of suggestions your way. Please don't get overwhelmed. During our journey together, I'll also be providing some specific guidance on how and at what pace to work these changes into your life.

$* * * * *$

To help you sift through the ideas I offer you, I'd like to suggest a very practical strategy to begin with:

It's a note-taking strategy.

It gives you permission to write in this book. To identify key points, perhaps you could put a star (*) next to all the ideas you like. Then, at the end of each chapter, go back and circle the two or three ideas you will commit to implement right now. Perhaps you divide your list into two categories: "doable now" and "doable...but later." Perhaps you can then transfer your final selections to sticky notes for your bathroom mirror or computer screen—where you will see them each day. This is just one suggestion to help anyone avoid feeling overwhelmed with all the suggestions in the book. If you have your own favorite method of identifying key points, feel free to use that instead.

Use whatever system works for you.

$* * * * *$

And now we will begin with the first step, where it all begins: our life of prayer and our relationship with the Lord Jesus from whom, through whom, and with whom all things are possible.

CHAPTER ONE

Prayer: Life in Relationship with the Lord

The Franciscan Friars of the Renewal talk about our holy father St. Francis and our holy mother St. Clare. But we also affectionately refer to Mother Teresa (St. Teresa of Calcutta) as our holy aunt Mother Teresa. Mother Teresa's life and work and the flourishing of her sisters greatly inspired our own founders. To this day, many of the friars look to her as a source of inspiration for their own vocations.

In many ways, Mother Teresa firmly became part of our family during her time visiting New York City to look for a suitable location to establish her first Missionaries of Charity convent in North America. Fr. Benedict Groeschel had the honor of aiding Mother Teresa in this search. At that time, the Friars of the Renewal had begun, but our foundation had not yet been set, and our rhythm and way of life were still being worked out.

During their various travels around the city, Mother Teresa asked Fr. Benedict about the friars and our way of life. As he began to share, it became very evident that Fr. Benedict and the friars were envisioning a life of radical mission and service, of preaching the gospel and loving the poor. An anecdotal account of the conversation between Fr. Benedict and Mother Teresa has been passed down over the years. It goes something like this:

Mother Teresa said, "Father, you need to make sure that your brothers make a holy hour every day."

Fr. Benedict looked at Mother Teresa and said, "Mother, I don't think we can do that. There's too much work to be done."

Mother Teresa, totally serious and without skipping a beat, said, "Well then, Father, make it two hours."

When St. Mother Teresa says something, we listen.

Prayer as Food

Why did Mother Teresa insist that the friars make a holy hour? And why, when we told her about how much work we were going to do, did she then up the ante and say pray more, not less? Because Mother Teresa knew what it took to begin a religious order and to be a source of renewal in the Church—she knew it must be a work of God. The friars are called to participate in God's renewal of all things. The renewal is God's. The rebuilding is God's. The victory is going to be the Lord's. But there will be no growth, there will be no new life, and there will be no victory without a deep commitment to prayer. Without God, we can do nothing, but with him, truly all things are possible.

Prayer is necessary. Prayer is a battle. Prayer is going to take some sacrifice and some work and some discipline, but prayer is beautiful and satisfying. We often refer to the interior life, the life of our relationship with the Lord, as the spiritual life. I think it's appropriate terminology, because it is a real life.

Let's reflect on the spiritual life in reference to natural life. There are many ways to end the natural life of a living being. Take the example of a rose. A rose can be killed by blunt trauma. It can be cut, stepped on, uprooted, or poisoned. Or a rose can be killed by negligence and neglect. If a rose is not watered, eventually it will die.

Likewise, there are a variety of ways in which one's spiritual life can die. It can be directly attacked through sin. This threat to the spiritual life is the most commonly talked about and focused on. But what could be even more dangerous, because of its subtlety and general acceptance in today's culture, is that the spiritual life can be killed simply by a lack of nourishment. It can be suffocated with distraction, anxiety, and concern about the world, or it can be starved by not being fed by a regular prayer life. Prayer is necessary to feed the soul. If we're not praying, we're dying.

I'd like that to be our first conviction and our first point of commitment and clarity. We need to pray. It is in prayer and our relationship with the Lord that we receive our daily bread, we receive guidance and strength for the journey, and we drink the living water that sustains us and nourishes us on our pilgrimage toward eternal life.

Obstacles to Prayer

During my time as a priest, I have had many conversations with sincere men and women who are trying to follow Jesus. Unfortunately, I find more often than not that they are struggling to pray with some consistency and depth. Can you relate? Many people say prayers here or there, but it is a very limited relationship. It may be keeping the spiritual life from dying, but it is certainly not nourishing the spiritual life enough for it to thrive. In this time and culture, we need thriving spiritual lives. We need a new generation of saints. In other words, we need a new generation of men and women of deep prayer. The men and women I speak with are sincere and good-willed; they know they should pray more and they even want to, but they don't. So let's dive into some of the challenges to prayer.

QUESTIONS FOR REFLECTION

How's my prayer life doing?

If I were to compare my prayer life to a natural life, would I say that it's being nourished and cultivated to the point of thriving? Or barely surviving? Or is it alive at all?

Do I believe in the value of prayer?

What are some of the obstacles that keep me from having a vibrant prayer life?

There are a lot of different obstacles to prayer, and we may face some more than others. We may have doubts about the real value of prayer. Maybe we're not convinced that it's fruitful and effective. Often our day-to-day responsibilities, which seem more pressing, capture our full focus. Maybe we're just distracted by so many other entertaining alternatives to prayer. Or maybe we've tried prayer and found it difficult. We don't know how to put together a prayer schedule. Even when we have some time for prayer, we don't really know what to do. We simply don't know *how* to pray. Let's take a look at these obstacles and how to overcome them.

"I JUST DON'T HAVE TIME"

I was in a group of friars traveling to Chicago from the Bronx to take part in an all-day video project. Judging by the production schedule, we could expect to be on the set for about twelve hours. I knew it was going to be a very long day, but I didn't know it was also going to be one of the most inspiring and influential experiences I'd have in my eleven years as a friar.

The night before the shoot, we were planning our schedule for the day. We had the production schedule, but we had to figure out our prayer schedule. Every day, along with our commitment to praying the Liturgy of the Hours, the friars attend or celebrate Mass and make a daily Eucharistic holy hour. We had a parish and Mass time selected. As we were discussing when we could make our holy hour, it became apparent to all of us that the only time that would work would have to be the hour before Mass. I immediately began thinking, "Maybe we should pass on making the holy hour today. We have an extremely long day, so it will be important for us to get all the rest we can." A reasonable idea!

The weight of the work schedule was beginning to sink in with one of the other friars as well. His conclusion, however, was very different. Quietly, almost to himself, he said, "Yeah, it's going to be a really long day. We're going to need that prayer time. … We'll need it to keep us going." He was right. He knew that our work, which was ultimately to be a spiritual work, would be empty if we did not pray.

I share that story to say I understand. I hear you. You have hundreds if not thousands of responsibilities and items on your to-do list. The demands of life are fast, taxing, and all over the place. So I would like you to take a look at your to-do list from a different perspective. I hear you saying something along the lines of, "All right, today I'm going to run a marathon." And I say, "Well then, make sure you get a good breakfast, and make sure you bring some food along to stay nourished and hydrated throughout the day."

When we say, "I don't have time for prayer because I'm too busy," it's like saying, "I don't have time to eat and drink because I have a marathon to run." I like this analogy because I think when we frame it this way, it makes a lot of sense. Feel free to replace "marathon" here with whatever image of a huge undertaking you can relate to. Whatever comparison you use, the message is the same: the more you have to do, the more important it is to pray.

It's reasonable and responsible to reflect on our lives to see if we are doing too much. We want our work to be building up the kingdom of God, and there's a temptation in today's world to commit to many different activities. Some are unnecessary, and some may even be coming from motivations we need to be concerned about. But ultimately, we hope that we're about God's work, and how are we going to be about God's work without God? Let's stop trying to run the marathon of life without proper nourishment.

QUESTIONS FOR REFLECTION

Am I living like a marathon runner with a big list of things I need to do without properly nourishing my spiritual life?

Are there commitments I've made and pursuits I'm committed to that maybe I can step back from?

Is activism suffocating my spiritual life?

Am I about God's work?

Am I convinced that I need God's help if I'm going to be about God's work? In fact, I need to be filled and nourished, guarded and guided by God.

"I NEED MOTIVATION"

An object in motion tends to stay in motion. We're moving fast, and the rhythms—our own established patterns of life and the rhythms of society—don't take into account the need for a prayer life. Society often doesn't value prayer. To pray every day and to pray throughout the day, we're going to need to make very firm commitments. We're going to need to stop the activism inertia; prayer has to be intentional and has to be active. Prayer has to be something that we commit to again and again and again.

A brother friar and I had just finished making our yearly solitude retreat with some cloistered nuns, and we had a chance at the end of the retreat to speak to one of these women of profound prayer. Our retreat had been up in the mountains with acres and acres of forest where it was still and quiet. Now we were going to be traveling back to the South Bronx.

The brother I was with asked one of the sisters, "It was so easy to pray here. This environment was ideal for entering into the stillness. How can we pray like this when we go back home?" And she looked at us with a warm and knowing smile and said, "Brothers, the creativity of love. When you love someone, you create a way to be with them."

My brothers and sisters, I would like to offer you an invitation to creative love. In your reflection on your day and your rhythm of life, can you create a space and a time to be with the Lord because you love him?

Again, we're going to need to make time for prayer. But I've become fond of saying that I think we can make some time for prayer—for God—if we start at ten minutes or fifteen minutes or thirty minutes. Because God literally made time for us, it seems right and just to make a little bit of time for God. It will be work, but it's worth it. May the Holy Spirit lead us and guide us. With the Holy Spirit's help, may we apply the creativity of love to our schedules, carving out space to be with our Beloved.

"IT'S A WASTE OF TIME"

If someone asks us, "Is prayer effective?" we would probably say yes. In theory, we say prayer is effective. But how deeply are we convinced that prayer is fruitful? How deeply are we convinced that prayer changes things? If we're honest with ourselves, many of us are going to wrestle with this area of faith. We're going to lean toward a self-reliance and an activism because we're not deeply convinced with all of our being that God is alive. We're not deeply convinced that God is in control and will bless and anoint and make fruitful our times of prayer.

I had a chance to live in our friary in Honduras for two years. Those were two of the greatest years of my religious life. As I started to learn more and more about the story of how we got there and the development of the Church in that area, the effectiveness of prayer became very obvious. About twenty years before the friars arrived in this little area, it was totally barren. There were no houses; there were no schools. There was nothing. It was in this barren, empty land that the bishop of the diocese planted a convent of cloistered nuns of the Poor Clare order. These sisters lived together and prayed together. They worshipped God, and they sacrificed for the good of the world, all behind closed doors. But their hidden life of prayer and sacrifice was not in vain. Actually, it would bear fruit in a way that was exceptional and experiential.

Fast forward thirty years. Within a five-hundred-yard radius where there once was nothing, there is now an orphanage for boys and an orphanage for girls. There is a hospital the friars run that gives totally free care to the poorest of the poor. There's a school for children with special needs. There's the friary, and there's our apostolic center, which is one of the most active apostolic centers in the entire country. There's a group of lay missionaries. I'm convinced that all these groups and houses and works of the Church, which are bringing healing and proclaiming the gospel of Christ and the identity of Jesus here, are the fruit of prayer. They are the fruit of the prayer and sacrifices of the hidden life of these Poor Clare women.

Staying in Relationship

Prayer is effective. Prayer changes things. I'd like to look at a couple of areas in which prayer can be effective in our lives. First of all, prayer is essential for keeping us rooted in reality—in the truth of who we are, who God is, how we got here, and where we're going. We can be too easily distracted from our goal and mission. We can easily make something a priority that is not a priority. And this distraction can make us forget that we're known and loved by God. We can forget that in each day and each moment, at all times, the loving gaze of the Father is upon us, loving us, rejoicing with us, supporting us, nourishing us, and encouraging us.

Life in relationship with the Lord is beautiful, and it's good. It's true, and it keeps us focused and grounded in reality. Prayer keeps us nourished by our Father's love for us.

Next, prayer is actually efficient because holiness is efficient. Sin, on the other hand, is radically inefficient. Think about how much work and stress we have to put into anxiety, whether it's from confusion or tension within our relationships or from wounds caused by our personal sins or the sins of another. Sin costs us a lot of time. Holiness, however, leads to peace, tranquility, clarity, truth, and unity. And if we persevere in prayer and grow in holiness, that time in prayer will actually bear fruit in the long run.

Jesus reminds us that anyone who gives up brothers or sisters or parents for his sake will receive a hundredfold in this life (see Matthew 19:29). A great example of this is a friend of the friars who is a prominent businessman. As a leader in a successful international company, he's got a lot of demands on his time and his schedule. At one point, he came to know the Lord, and he began to pray. He ended up developing the habit of praying three rosaries a day, which takes about forty or forty-five minutes. When asked if he ever has to pray less, he says he needs to pray three rosaries a day because when he's praying, he knows the Lord goes before him. And the Lord takes care of things, bringing healing, efficiency, and clarity. If he doesn't pray those three rosaries a day, he feels like he loses time because there are new problems that he has to solve. His lived experience is that when he prays, he actually has more time.

QUESTIONS FOR REFLECTION

Are there areas of my life where I tend toward self-sufficiency? Are there areas where I don't pray because I really doubt that God will take care of me and take care of my needs?

Are there some ways in which I've experienced the fruitfulness of prayer? Could I remember those times as a source of inspiration and encouragement to pray in the future?

DISTRACTIONS

My hypothesis is that the primary reason most people are not praying is just simply distraction. Especially with the innovation of the smartphone, there's always something easier to do than pray. We can always turn on the radio or the TV or scroll through the phone; there's an unlimited source of entertaining distractions. The problem with all these distractions is they're like sugar for the soul. They're enjoyable and even addicting at some points, but they don't bring complete nourishment. In fact, if we maintain a diet of only sugar, it eventually could contribute to rotting teeth and illness, right? But what if we're willing to step away from some of the "sugar"—some of the entertainment and noise and distraction of sports or news or politics or other hobbies? If, instead, we move toward cultivating our life of prayer, I know we'll find something much deeper and more satisfying than soul sugar.

I mentioned earlier the cloistered nuns in Honduras who did the spiritual work that created such a fruitful and thriving environment. I had a chance to visit them with a cameraman to help them with some promotional materials. We were invited to experience their life in about a three-hour span. In this time, I got to see more or less the entire grounds of their convent. Again, these are cloistered nuns, which means they never leave the space. By my estimate, the distance from the very front to the very back of their cloister—which in the physical sphere is their whole world—is about equal to how far I could throw a baseball. Probably not a football, but I could definitely hit a sand wedge over it. In other words, it's a small space.

I reflected on the fact that the sisters never leave this physical ground. And what dawned on me is that these women and their joy in their cloistered life is a profound witness to the real depth of the interior journey. The spiritual life—the journey with the Lord within one's own heart—is profoundly beautiful, as beautiful as any mountain range. It has jewels as brilliant as any diamond. But most of us have never tasted the sweetness of profound prayer or a profound spiritual life, and so—not knowing what we're missing—we too readily settle for the easy and the easily accessible.

I'd like to invite you to give prayer a chance, at least for a period of time. Make a commitment to some times of deep prayer, or make a commitment to times focused just on prayer and quiet in the Lord. I'm convinced that you will taste and see that the Lord is good. I'm convinced that you'll develop a taste for prayer and that you'll want to pray. Prayer is like filet mignon and lobster tail for the soul. Much of the entertainment and social commentary we spend our time consuming is like colorful candy for the soul. We like our candy! But the more we acquire the taste for the spiritual surf and turf, the more easily we'll not "spoil our dinner" by indulging in lesser distractions.

QUESTIONS FOR REFLECTION

Is my view of prayer motivated more by love or by obligation?

Have I ever thought that prayer might be sweet and fulfilling and satisfying in a way that I haven't experienced before?

Do I believe I can have a real relationship with God and really experience his love?

What are some of the distractions in my life that are keeping me from prayer?

"WHAT DO I DO?"

Another obstacle for men and women of good will that keeps them from praying and eventually leads to a malnourished spiritual life is simply not knowing how to pray. In the Church, we do have a great blessing of formal prayer. We know how to go to Mass and listen to the homily, and we pray the Rosary, but sometimes our understanding of prayer hasn't really moved beyond that. So unfortunately, we can get bored or distracted by prayer very quickly. I had this experience in high school when I became involved in youth ministry. One of the women volunteers invited me to make a visit to the Blessed Sacrament chapel. There were a couple of us, and we went in, and I knelt down. I said an Our Father, a Hail Mary, and a Glory Be, and then I was done. I just didn't know what else to do outside of these basic formal prayers. I'd never been taught to pray.

That's the experience for many of us. We have limited our understanding of prayer to saying formal prayers instead of entering into relationship and intimacy and conversation with the Lord.

Prayer Is Conversation

One of my most powerful lessons in prayer came from a friend's dad. He's a normal dad with a normal job whose work commute was about an hour each way. On that drive to and from work, he would invite the guidance of the Holy Spirit. He would visualize and recognize the reality that God was with him. He would talk to God and share with him his feelings, his thoughts, his concerns, his needs, and his joys and sorrows, as he would if his best friend were sitting in the passenger seat. He'd simply talk to God as you would to a friend.

So how does one learn to pray? There are many books on prayer that are extremely helpful, of course, but for the scope of this book, I'd simply like to invite you to experiment with prayer as a conversation between you and the One you love—you and your best friend. Have this conversation to grow in your capacity to share your heart and your dreams and your fears and your anxieties with the Lord. Share your pains, your sorrows, and your successes with him. You can do this in the chapel, in the car, through journaling, or in other ways. God deeply wants to hear from you. He deeply wants to have this relationship with you and speak with you.

QUESTIONS FOR REFLECTION

When I think of praying, do I have an understanding of prayer or experience of prayer outside of formal prayers?

Can I talk to Jesus as a friend, to God as my Father who loves me and wants to hear from me? Can I share with him my fears, my sorrows, my hopes, and my dreams?

Spiritual Meal Prep

When would be a good time to practice prayer? What should a prayer schedule look like? The answer is that the rhythm of prayer and the way of prayer is going to be unique for each one of us. It might change with different times or seasons.

What I propose as nonnegotiable is that each of us needs to have some time for prayer. Each day we need our nourishment. I'd also like to propose ways of sanctifying not only our day but also our week, our month, and our year.

The friars are committed to sanctifying each day with a minimum of about four hours of prayer. A central part of that is our praying of the Liturgy of the Hours, which we do in common five times a day. We have Mass every morning, Eucharistic holy hour every evening, and then the Rosary with night prayer before we call it a night. Understand, we're religious, and our life gives us some freedom to do this type of prayer. Most people won't be able to pray for hours a day, especially with demands of work or school or kids, but I bet you'd be surprised how much time you can pray if you really want it.

SANCTIFY YOUR DAY

So the first principle is simply this: Sanctify your day. Each day, have some time of prayer in the morning. If you're not praying at all, I would say a minimum of five minutes is a great first step. It might be time to read the Gospel reading of the day. It might be time to make a daily offering, to entrust your day to God and speak to him from the heart about what you have on your plate: what your anxieties are, what you're nervous about, what you need to do, your relationships, who you're going to be with, who you're going to see. Start your day with prayer.

If you think about it, no one's going to play a basketball game or go into a meeting at work or go on a road trip without a plan or without fuel in the tank. We all frequently make plans for how to get to our goals or achieve our tasks, but so often we go about the most important journey without a plan and without fuel. It's the most obvious thing in the world to me that we need to begin each day with prayer. That way, we go into our day with a plan and with the resources and the tools we need to thrive.

Second, a little moment of prayer at midday is a great thing to do. What I think would be helpful and practical for almost anybody is what I call the three-by-five examen.[2] You take five minutes and reflect on your day. You give gratitude to God for five things that have already happened in the day. You ask his mercy for five things you think you could have done better; maybe you sinned. Then you entrust to him five things that are going to come with the second half of the day and ask for his guidance. The three-by-five examen takes five minutes to reorient us and reroute us to reality. It's a great way to remain nourished and to be re-energized as we go about the second part of our day.

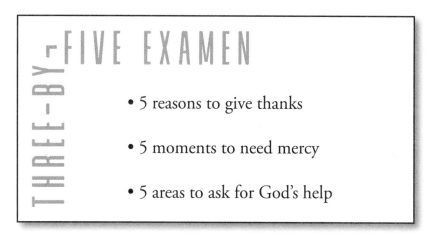

THREE-BY-FIVE EXAMEN

- 5 reasons to give thanks

- 5 moments to need mercy

- 5 areas to ask for God's help

Then finally, look back and reflect in the evening. I think that any active and healthy spiritual life will include a daily examination of conscience. Take some time to look back on your day, focusing especially on the ways you have experienced God's presence and blessing. Give him thanks for the successes, entrust to him the people you've met, and ask his mercy for areas where you failed. Then ask for his grace to begin the next day with his guidance and his spirit.

In the great tradition of so many religious orders, the evening is also a beautiful time to have a little word with Our Lady. It could be the Rosary, or it could be the Hail Mary or Hail, Holy Queen or your favorite Marian prayer. It's a beautiful and laudable tradition to end your day this way, perhaps with an image of Our Lady in your house, entrusting yourself to her maternal care.

SANCTIFY YOUR WEEK

Each week, the friars have what we call a prayer day; other traditions call it a desert day or hermitage day. It's one day out of the week when we take a step aside from some of our apostolic demands to focus on prayer and our relationship with the Lord. We're all in the midst of the world, and it makes sense that some of the world will stick to us like dust to the feet of a weary traveler. If we're going to be saints in the midst of the world at our places of work, in our schools, in our culture, and in our media, we're going to pick up some of the dust. That's going to start to hamper us in our understanding of who God is and why we exist and what our mission is. It's going to tempt us toward sin and distract us. So it's a good, laudable practice to make a little extra time each week in our schedule for prayer.

For the friars it's a day, and again, that's one of the great privileges of our religious life and one of the fruits of a life of celibacy. But can you get an extra hour, maybe on a Saturday morning, to go to Mass, to spend an hour in front of the Blessed Sacrament, or to do spiritual reading? You're invited to practice your creative love in the situation where you find yourself. Can you try each week to have one period of time that is more dedicated to prayer or spiritual reading—to shaking off some of the dust?

SANCTIFY YOUR MONTH

Each month, the friars take a forty-eight-hour hermitage time in which we leave the city and go to a retreat center to spend an extended period of time in prayer. The rationale is similar to the prayer day. We're in the midst of the world with all its different demands and confusing messages. And to make sure we stay focused and stay fed, we very intentionally and strategically have this prayer time each month to rest, refocus, and be renewed by the Lord.

Can you find a way to sanctify your month? Perhaps for one morning or one afternoon—just one each month—have an even more dedicated time for things with the Lord. It can be a time of prayer or ongoing spiritual reading or meeting with a small group of peers or doing an activity with your family. Perhaps it could be having a spiritual conversation. Perhaps it could be visiting another church. If there's a mission church or something like that in your area, visit that. Just once a month for a couple of hours at the least, find a time to go even deeper and be more dedicated to the Lord in the spiritual life.

SANCTIFY YOUR YEAR

I know this next proposal is challenging, but I'd ask you not to dismiss it out of hand. In our own rhythm of life, again made possible by the luxury of being religious, the friars make two one-week retreats each year. It's a time of extensive focus on prayer and recommitment. Often a friar will get a word for the year, have a chance to reflect on the past year, and find guidance for what the Lord wants to do in his life going forward in the next year. I think there's a wisdom to it, which can be applied to the life of the laity.

Can you make a longer retreat? What the retreat looks like can be creative. It can be a formal retreat, or it can be time away with your family or a small group of friends, time just dedicated to the Lord and to prayer.

I like to reflect back on the example of the cloistered nuns who don't have to travel and see the world physically because of how deeply and how well they're experiencing the journey in the spiritual life. And if we've tasted and seen the goodness of the Lord and the profound depths and vistas of the spiritual life, we would be much more urgent about scheduling time for retreat. By being wise, prudent, and forward thinking, can we create a life and a schedule that will allow us to get a weekend dedicated to the Lord? That time will be an opportunity to reflect back on the year with the Lord and to ask his guidance for the year going forward.

QUESTIONS FOR REFLECTION

How can I sanctify my day?

How can I sanctify my week?

How can I sanctify my month?

How can I sanctify my year?

I will write this down and share it with my husband or wife if I am married, or with a friend, roommate, or small group. If I have a plan and share it, it will bear fruit.

CHAPTER TWO

Family: The Power of Relationship

Let's begin this chapter by picking a little fight. There is a much-loved and often-quoted statement taken from Fyodor Dostoyevsky that "beauty will save the world."[3] It's a really nice saying. It makes you feel good. It's filled with hope. It's cute, even beautiful. It's safe. But is it true? It's a statement that I have been thinking about now for years, first as an early adopter and now with some reservations.

The Catholic Faith has a tremendous patrimony of artists. Art is integral to our worship of God and our experience of God—because art is integral to our humanity, and our humanity is integral to our spirituality. But instead of getting fully behind the idea that beauty will save the world, I'd like to propose what I believe to be a more true position: Family will save the world.

Our Movement Toward Relationship

The experience of beauty magnifies the glory of God and makes it experiential. It is pivotal in piercing the heart, breaking through, and softening the soul. For many people, it is literally the beauty of the liturgy that broke them open and brought them to the Lord. This is why beauty is often referred to as the spearhead of evangelization.

Yet beauty is only an instrument, a means to an even deeper end. The evangelical power of beauty is that it draws us into a relationship with God. Perhaps I feel so strongly about this because I know in my own life that what I most deeply crave is not beautiful music or a solitary hour in front of a masterpiece. It is not life at the threshold of some of nature's great beauties, like mountains and oceans. I appreciate and will actively seek out these things, but what I most deeply desire at the end of the day is relationship. What I most deeply desire is intimacy. What I most deeply desire is to be in communion with others. In other words, what I most deeply desire is family.

When I was a young teenager still very much trying to figure out who I was and where I was going, I found a home in the Catholic Church because I experienced family in the Catholic Church. I was welcomed day in and day out by those at the church who took me as another son or nephew or brother. It was these relationships that brought me into the church. It was my relationship with the church community that brought me into relationship with the Trinity.

We're all headed to the same place. We're all made for eternal communion with God and one another. We're all made for the fullest expression of intimacy and communion and union and family. We call that heaven, where we as brothers and sisters will be united in the loving gaze and presence of our heavenly Father.

Our Movement Away from Relationship

It is not simply beauty that will save the world. It is the beauty of family that will save us and sustain us. Before we get into the details, I'd like to take a moment to look at some of the mechanics of human relationships. I'd like to do so in reference to the natural world.

I'm by no stretch a scientist or a physicist. But it's my understanding, speaking broadly, that the theory of the big bang came from scientists watching the movement of the celestial bodies. The universe is expanding. There is this constant movement of the celestial bodies away from each other.

Through the years, as scientists observed this movement and studied the principles behind it, they realized that there must have been a moment when this movement began, and they theorized that there was a unity that exploded and created this constant movement. The explosion is referred to as the big bang, hence the big bang theory.

But also there is gravity. Matter is naturally drawn. Objects of matter are naturally drawn to other objects of matter. There is a universal attraction. All of us and all physical bodies experience these two consistent but contrary movements, movement away and attraction toward.

I begin with this physical observation because I think it speaks very eloquently to what we all experience interiorly. We're all drawn to one another. We desire friendship. We desire intimacy. We want to be known and loved. It's part of the God-given desire for heaven. We were made for communion with one another and communion with God. At the same time, we all struggle with one another. We are inclined toward isolation and selfishness and away from neighbor and God. We experience concupiscence (a tendency toward sin and isolation), which we can see as the inertia of the spiritual big bang of original sin.

It's important to identify these two consistent but contrary movements at the beginning. Why? Because they are universal and because the choice for communion will always be a choice. That's the reality of our human experience. The inertia of concupiscence is like a stream, and the movement toward communion is like rowing up that stream. It requires work. It requires an active choice. Often it can become tiresome, but we're made for it and we need it. We want it.

If I am counseling a young man or woman, the first step is always to get these two essentials locked in: prayer and family (committed community). Prayer is like the water and sunlight to the rose. Family is like the soil. We need both.

QUESTIONS FOR REFLECTION

Can I identify in myself these two movements, one toward isolation and selfishness and the other toward communion and relationship?

Am I in touch with my desire for family? At the same time, am I in touch with my desire to escape and isolate and self-medicate?

Am I aware of the reality that I am made for heaven, which is the most intense and eternal communal relationship?

Have I experienced the beauty of the Catholic Faith by experiencing it as family?

God at Work in Us Through Relationships

The Church really is the mystical body of Christ, and Christ continues to really work through his mystical body. The ordinary movement of the Holy Spirit is always toward union and communion, whereas the ordinary movement of sin is always toward division and isolation. God is trying to bring about this communion and form us into one family. But he's ordinarily going to do so through human instruments—through other people. It shouldn't be too much of a leap to appreciate this if we look at our own lives and our own families. We see the ways they have formed us and enriched and challenged us—and sometimes even hurt us.

We can't ignore the profound way in which the people we live with and interact with affect us. But we often divorce those experiences from God and his work and his plan. Entering religious life, this truth hit me hard. I come from a great family, I had a great group of friends, and I always had a deep desire for brotherhood. I also had a real and sincere life of prayer. It was within my life of prayer that

I experienced God and heard his voice and received the grace to respond. When I entered religious life, there was this great moment of enlightenment when I realized that my relationship with the Lord and my relationships with others are not two separate worlds. They are very much one, and I realized that my following of the Lord would be deeply integrated into my life of community.

The community would not just be a source of friendship and external support and accountability. Through my brothers, God would get his hands dirty in the re-creation of my heart and my soul, of the entire new man.

Vulnerability

One of the first moments I experienced this reality poignantly was when I was a postulant. Postulancy, when I entered religious life, was the first six-month period. In postulancy, a man would begin to wade into the waters of religious life, leave the world, and begin to be formed in this new way of life. I somewhat jokingly (but not totally jokingly) refer to the hardest day of postulancy—the hardest day of radically giving my life to Jesus—as the first time I had to sing in front of others.

I was a sports guy, and I spent my whole childhood basically playing land sports. I was not a singer. I had never sung in front of a person, not by myself. That day was my day to lead a hymn at the start of evening prayer. About an hour and a half before, as the moment approached, the anxiety kicked in. I became short of breath and really nervous. My palms were sweating, and my breathing was restricted. I asked one of the brothers, "Is it possible just to recite it?" The brother said, "No, that's not going to work." So I practiced and practiced and listened and listened. But again, I was starting from scratch.

So the big moment came when I had to sing in front of my new brothers, the other fifteen or so men in the chapel. Through my restricted windpipe and dried-up mouth, I gave it my best shot. I guess I blew out some air and some higher decibels, and maybe you could call it singing, though not many people would. But I got through it.

Later I reflected on it. You know what happened with the brothers after I failed miserably to sing in front of them—these men I looked up to, whose respect I wanted? You know what happened? Nothing. They didn't change their behavior toward me at all. They didn't reject me.

As I look back on this moment, I view it as a mystery. Why was I so afraid to sing in front of them? In my years of processing this moment, I realized that up to this point I had never had to be weak and vulnerable in front of a group of people I deeply respected. I was good at sports, so I played sports. I was not good at singing, so I didn't sing. In the past, I'd had a great deal of control over my world and my community. So I could even choose where I was vulnerable and where I let people in. But now that I had given my life to this family—to this committed and intimate communion—I would no longer be able to hide, and I would no longer be able to control all that.

Merciful Love

When I was careful only to meet people in my strengths—when I showed them the straight As on my report card or the sports trophy—I received their admiration and respect. They saw that I was good at something, and they respected it, noted it, and responded to it. But that is a very shallow experience of love and relationship. When I entered religious life and consistently allowed my brothers to experience me in my weakness and my struggle and my failure and even my sin and selfishness, I experienced a much more profound level of love. I experienced the type of love one might call mercy. In my weakness and in their mercy, I had a brand-new experience of love and a new insight into myself.

I knew that my failures did not define me. I knew that I didn't have to fear rejection. I knew that I was known and loved even in my weakness, my incapacity, my ongoing and not-healing sin. And I came to know this not at the theoretical but at the experiential level. I experienced my brothers knowing me and loving me. In my brothers knowing me and loving me, I experienced the Father's knowledge and love of me. As I was a beggar before my brothers, begging for their mercy and their patience, I received the capacity to be generous with my brothers and sisters who themselves were in need of mercy or patience or compassion.

It was in the stuff of committed community that I experienced this insight into God. Many of us, even in our families, are still in control and still able to hide our weakness and our struggle. The difficulty is that we end up limiting our experience of love. We control how much others know of us and so limit the depth to which we know their love.

We're all in need of a merciful love. We're all loved with a merciful love. God wants us to experience this. He wants to encourage us and enlighten us and enrich us with this love in the context of Christian family.

QUESTIONS FOR REFLECTION

Have I experienced being loved in my weakness and known in my weakness by others?

Am I afraid of it?

Are there ways in which I control my environment to make sure no one ever sees me in my struggle or my difficulty?

Do I desire to be known and loved through and through in my strengths and *weaknesses, in what I am proud of in myself and what I am terrified of in myself?*

Are there any ways I think God might be desiring to give me an experience of his love in my family or in my community?

Are there any ways I actively flee from or hide from the Lord to avoid giving him the space to give me this gift?

Prayer as Love's Forge

Anybody who has been in any sort of community, whether in a family or at school or at work, is very much in touch with some of the difficulties that come with living with other people. In this next section, I'd like to be honest about some of the difficulties of living in a family. And I'd also like to talk about the ways even these difficulties are good news that can be salvific.

Let's look at how a sword is made. I love this image as a way to understand how God forms us. The blacksmith takes the rough piece of steel and sets it in the fire, where it stays until it becomes glowing hot. Then the blacksmith removes the steel from the fire and hits it with a hammer to shape it and form it into a sword.

This process is repeated over and over again until the sword is sparkling and sharp, beautiful and whole. I often see community life and God's work of forming us in this light. The fire that we must continuously enter and rest in is the fire of God, the relationship we have with the Lord. We need to keep praying and so keep entering into this relationship. I can't overemphasize the importance of this prayer, this time in the fire of God's love and God's truth. It makes the blows of life and the blows of community formative and not the means of injury.

The hammer is going to fall; the blows are going to come. It's the nature of living in a fallen world as a fallen person among other fallen men and women. If we do not pray—if we are hit by these blows but we have not been made docile by the fire of God's love and God's truth—the blows will wound us and hurt us. They will not be formative, just painful. But if we remain in relationship with the Lord, these blows will form us and make us stronger as they come. They will actually be the means by which God can form us into who we are made to be.

The Hammer Blows of Community Life

Living as a friar over the last decade, I've experienced community life as a hammer blow a number of times. It's going to happen even in the best of families or religious communities. Where there are different people, there are going to be differences and disagreements. Where there are human beings, there are going to be hammer blows! I'm sure you can think of countless examples in your own experiences as a member of a family, team, or other group.

I'd like to share a fairly mild example but one which I believe many of you will find relatable. The friars have the tradition of praying a voluntary communal Rosary in the evening. After night prayer, those who wish can stay and pray the Rosary together. If you're not careful, praying this Rosary can sometimes feel like a battle. Each of us has his own internal speed and temperament. Some prefer to pray very slowly, and some prefer to pray very fast. It's a moment when six to ten of us have to pray at one speed in one rhythm. If you lose perspective, the fact that not everyone wants to pray at the pace at which you're most comfortable can become a great annoyance and can even feel like an obstacle to prayer.

The challenge is to see the diversity as an opportunity to grow in unity. God is at work in these details. God is at work in the need to yield to the preference of another so that we can keep one rhythm and one voice as part of the movement of growing in one heart and one mind. The fight to become one in pace is not an obstacle to the prayer. It is really a very hands-on way in which the Lord is forming us and making us one. The slow brother may feel like a hammer blow to the fast brother and vice versa, but if we're staying in relationship, these become holy hammer blows. They really form us!

The Choice Between Me and Us

I think we have all had these types of experiences, whether it's what TV show we're going to watch, what we're going to eat, where we're going to eat, or how fast we're going to drive. The temptation is always to divorce these real struggles and real experiences from God's work. We label them as obstacles to holiness or obstacles to happiness or communion. But in fact, if we prayerfully invite God into these moments, we see that they are the real nitty-gritty.

If we continue to invite the Lord into these moments and allow grace to protect our perspective, we'll see that we are in fact in God's workshop. It is in the war in the living room (for the remote) or at the dinner table or in the car that he is forming us. In these moments, he is inviting us to choose the good of another over our own good. He's inviting us to die to our own preferences. It is in these moments that we are making that authentic exodus of love, the journey from me to you. If our relationship with the Lord remains just "me and him" and not "us and him," then we can basically write whatever narrative we want to. That is the struggle and the temptation for all of us.

When we isolate ourselves, God very quickly becomes conformed to our own image, and our own image is conformed to some inauthentic model that we're forming out of context with reality. When we are in relationship with others, we are forced to see who we really are before them, before ourselves, and before God. Similarly, it's in relationship with the Church that we're protected from transforming God into our own image of him.

Things to Do as a Family

I'd like to get into some practical details about how to live in communion. First, we all need to make sure that we are always being made formable by the fire of the Father's love. We have to *keep praying.* Community life will kill us if it is divorced from a real, lived relationship with the Lord. It will kill us if we're not able to see God's hand and God's work in the midst of the details and circumstances of our lives.

We also have to take time to recognize and *understand the two different movements in our lives:* the movement away from community, toward self and isolation, and the movement toward relationship, the felt desire for communion. We have to own the reality that it probably will cost us, some of us more than others, to keep entering into relationship, to work at it, and to remain in it.

We do a couple of things in the friary that you can model and apply in your own life. First, pray about and *fight for a nightly dinner together* every single night, at the same time, in the same place, eating the same food together. It can be difficult to set up as everyone tries to sync up different schedules and preferences. It is in this initial moment and in this dynamic that we're doing the work and allowing God to do the work of forming us into one.

It can be difficult, but it's really essential that we take back the family dinner. A family dinner might look like many different things for different families. At this point, we're proposing an ideal with the understanding that it may take some time to get there, but at least we know where we're headed. At least we can begin praying for that or having conversations leaning in that direction. Of course, many people are involved in putting together a family dinner, and it may not be easy to manufacture this new lifestyle overnight.

We just have to make the commitment to actually have a family dinner. Situations vary. Ideally, it's every day. In the friary, we do not have a recreation time; we have speaking dinners instead, as opposed to dinner where readings take place, which is common in other monastic situations. And we don't have TV or radio or music in the friary, so those things aren't a temptation. Not having them creates the space and the time.

Because dinner is scheduled, we know we're going to be there for an hour. We don't rush. We're there. We sit back; we relax. We share stories. We talk about how we're doing. We talk about who we've met along the way. It creates this great opportunity for us to be with one another and build each other up.

Another thing about dinner together: If there are tensions, you have to stay in the relationship. Instead of letting the tensions fester or escaping from them, you have to work through them, because you know you'll be at dinner together.

If your family is not already doing this every night, probably the first best step will be to pray about it. The second best step will be to talk to the others about it and to explain why it's so important to you. And then begin to apply it as it works. You'll want these dinners to be without distraction, so no TVs, no music, no cell phones. Dinner is just the time to be together, all the while recognizing and understanding the inclination we all have to want to be on our own. That is the cost. But the value of being together and experiencing a living family is necessary and essential.

Another recommendation is to *find opportunities to serve one another.* It might be as simple as filling up another's glass, or it might be serving food or cooking a homemade meal instead of ordering in. All these are different ways in which I'm able to serve you and you're able to serve me. These small moments create a culture. They are moments of grace and of unity, and essentially they are steps toward God's kingdom coming here and now.

Another way to build community is by beginning to practice *honoring one another.* For many of us, honoring someone else can be uncomfortable. We didn't grow up speaking from the heart in a vulnerable way, especially not in front of others in a communal setting. But doing so is an essential practice for building each other up and promoting healing in our communities and families.

Within the friary we don't particularly celebrate birthdays, but we each have a feast day that we celebrate. It's a long-established custom to honor a brother on his feast day. When we're all together, we go around and each of us honors the brother for some virtue, thanks him for his friendship, or acknowledges another way in which he has enriched us by his presence.

It's a beautiful way as a family to very intentionally have a time where we speak truth into the lives of other people. The fact that we're all doing it and that it's organized helps with some of the fear of the intimacy if we're not accustomed to it. But it also can be a place of tremendous healing, especially for tensions or frustrations. If I'm the one being honored, it's a way for me to hear that each of the others really does love me, care for me, and see something good in me. It's incredibly healing.

QUESTIONS FOR REFLECTION

Beyond the occasional wedding toast or Thanksgiving "go around the table and say what you're thankful for," what are some ways my family and I can practice honoring one another? How might that look in my life?

How might that look with my spouse?

How might that look with my children?

How might that look in my workplace?

Could it be part of a celebration of friends at a birthday party? Wherever you find community, see if you can introduce this healing, loving practice.

CHAPTER THREE

Catholic Culture and Liturgical Living: More Than Patches

Frank Sheed, a popular Catholic author and publisher of the twentieth century, once wrote that Catholics today don't have Catholic minds so much as "worldly minds with Catholic patches."[4] I think something similar can be said about Catholics and culture. Often we don't have Catholic culture or Catholic homes so much as worldly culture and worldly homes with Catholic patches.

In this chapter we're going to take a look at our personal, familial, and societal cultures to see if they're truly Catholic and, if not, what we can do. First, we'll take a look at what culture is and why it is important. Then we'll use a few images to help us understand the effects of culture on our growth. And finally, we'll get particular and look at specific ways we can build our own Catholic cultures. We'll look especially at our conversation, our family dinners, what we do on Fridays, and most importantly, our Sundays.

What Culture Is

One of my most fascinating insights into human culture and, in some ways, the culture where it is now has come from driving past Yankee Stadium in the South Bronx on the way back from Sunday Mass at a convent. If the Yankees are in town, the traffic pattern is radically changed as I weave my way back to the friary: Traffic and police are everywhere. All over the South Bronx, tens of thousands of people are dressed up wearing Yankees hats and jerseys and waving Yankees pennants in the air. They're spending hours and hours at the game and, many times, hundreds and hundreds of dollars. To them, being a Yankees fan is a huge part of their culture and who they are. It affects their schedules, pocketbooks, and moods—and it affects traffic like you wouldn't believe. On game day it affects what they wear and what they eat. Their fandom can't just be kept in—it's expressed. Their love creates a culture.

So what is culture and why is it so important? Culture is where the rubber hits the road. It's where our hearts become manifest in our actions. It's a mirror of our values. Our personal cultures include how we spend our time, how we spend our money, and what we understand to be morally right and wrong. It is also how we fundamentally, existentially understand the world, our relationships with one another, and our relationship with God.

QUESTIONS FOR REFLECTION

How deeply does my Catholic faith permeate my life? Do I really understand that I have a loving Father and am made for eternity?

Do I value spiritual goods above all else?

And do I really accept the reality that we belong to one another and are meant to love and care for one another, especially those who are the most vulnerable?

Is our Catholic faith like leaven, mixed in and giving life to every aspect of what we do, what we say, and our approach to the world? Or is it more like chocolate chips baked into a cookie? They're there, they're substantial, and you can see them, but many parts of the dough have not been touched by them. Or maybe our faith is just sprinkles, an exterior topping that hasn't really gotten into the stuff of our life.

This topic is of particular interest to me because, really, the turning point of my life was when I discovered the answer. As a young man, I had this idea that I wanted to be dynamic. Being dynamic meant having a little bit of everything. It was a compartmentalized life. I wanted to go to church, absolutely, but I didn't want to get crazy about it. And I wanted to help the poor, but it would be here and there. I also wanted to experience and live many of the values that were common to other college kids, including parties and immorality. I wanted to be well rounded. And of course, I wanted Jesus to be involved in my life, but again, I didn't want to get crazy with it. I didn't want to be radical.

I wanted to believe and was willing to believe and did believe, but I didn't want to take it too far.

Then one day in college, I was just hanging out with a group of friends, and I got to speaking to a young lady I hadn't met before. She said she was an atheist. Immediately I began proposing the Faith and defending the Faith to her, spurred on, honestly, by a little liquid courage. And as I was defending the authority of Scripture and the reality of God, sharing my disbelief that someone could actually not believe, the Holy Spirit came and ripped my heart wide open. The words he inscribed on my heart and my mind and my lips have radically changed the entire trajectory of my life: "You believe, and it needs to affect everything."

Faith and Culture

The truth of our faith and the beauty and goodness of it are meant to affect everything. At this point, I'm going to ask you not to run too far ahead in your thoughts about what this might mean and take it to extreme lengths. We will slowly unpack what it means to allow the Faith to touch everything. It may also be helpful to approach it from another direction.

If people believe that there is a creating God who loves them to the point that he sent his only-begotten Son to die for them so that they could be with him forever, does it make sense for their lives and homes and families to look exactly like everyone else's? Wouldn't their lives look different from the lives of people who believe that there is no meaning in life, that life is simply the result of accidents, that there is not anything beyond this life?

Our values as Catholics are radically different. And at least intellectually, we understand that this should mean that our lives look radically different. But do they? Is what we watch on TV and how we use the internet radically different? Is how we understand our poor and suffering brothers and sisters radically different? Are the ways we spend our time, have conversations, think, and plan different because they have been touched by the radical love and truth of our beautiful faith?

If you're reading this book, your faith is probably not sprinkles on top of the cookie. It's probably like chocolate chips at least, pretty baked in. You're probably committed to Sunday Mass. And Christmas is not just about the presents, but you believe and give thanks for the gift of Jesus. At Easter, I'm sure the highlight is not the Easter egg hunt but the celebration of the risen Christ. But let's take a look and see if there's a way for our faith to affect our lives even more deeply.

QUESTIONS FOR REFLECTION

Are there areas in my life that have not been touched by my faith in Jesus?

If someone who had only read about Christianity visited my home or looked at my playlist or my bank statements, would that person see a reflection there of what they had read?

Does my life look radically different from the lives of those who do not hold the same beliefs as mine?

Culture as a Greenhouse

At this point, I'd like to take a look at culture using the image of a greenhouse, which was introduced to me by Michelle and Chris Benzinger, who run the Greenhouse Collective. The idea is that to heal plants, you don't directly apply medicine to the plant itself, but you check its soil. Often, what is most needed is a change of soil and atmosphere. It's the purpose of a greenhouse to provide an ideal environment for the plant to heal and grow and bear fruit. The Benzingers' Greenhouse Collective aims to do this for people.

We are trying to live holiness in the midst of the world, and our experiences in the world may harm what God is trying to grow within us. This is one reason why our personal and family cultures are so important. They are meant to protect us, heal us, and reorient us when the world confuses us and tempts us away from God.

One time I experienced the wounding effect of culture was when I was a postulant and we had the opportunity to visit the family home of one of the friars. It was a Sunday afternoon. They were big Patriots fans, and the game was on in the background. For a few minutes, I sat down and watched the game. Within about ten minutes, I experienced something of a crisis of faith or of lifestyle, to speak about it dramatically.

The game set up a mirror in my mind in which I suddenly saw myself differently. The game was celebrating human athleticism, material wealth, and physical beauty. And I looked at myself and what I was doing in that mirror, and for a moment I was almost embarrassed, like, "What am I doing with my life?" On the way back to the friary that evening, we prayed our Rosary, and back at the friary I spent time chatting with the friars. Then we went into night prayer, and I spent time with Jesus in the Blessed Sacrament. And slowly but surely, that little wound and those little lies that were trying to take root in my life were dissipated by the light of Christ, the goodness of our fraternal life, and the knowledge that my life was at the service of the gospel, especially my poor brothers and sisters. But that wounding also showed me the radical power of the culture to speak into my life in unexpected ways.

That is happening to us all with our coworkers, what we watch on TV, what we read, and what we look at when we're using the computer. These experiences communicate values and worldviews. They hold up mirrors to us that may challenge or belittle our Catholic values. If we are not firmly protected and surrounded by the light of Christ in our own personal cultures—if we are not rooted in the truth of Christ—they will wound us. They can sometimes poison us and even threaten our faith.

A healthy Catholic culture is going to remind us of what we believe and why we believe. It will surround us and protect us. It's going to give us a place to experience again and again the beauties of our faith. It's going to remind us of our dignity as sons and daughters of the most loving Father.

QUESTIONS FOR REFLECTION

Do my family and I experience home as a greenhouse, as a place where we are healed of lies and renewed in the goodness of God?

Am I aware of ways in which my interactions with others, with the media, or with material things are affecting my worldview? Am I understanding of myself and my God?

Enriching Our Relationships

Wherever we live and work and study, we're creating culture when we act. It may be in our family or at college or in a religious community. Here are some ways to create culture.

SPIRITUAL CONVERSATION

One way we can create Catholic culture is through spiritual conversation. There's a growing cache of research and anecdotal evidence supporting the hypothesis that the most important factor for children to keep their faith once they leave the home is whether or not they had regular spiritual conversations with their parents.[5] The Lord is not going to be the center of our lives or the lives of our children if he is not occasionally the center of the conversation.

What are spiritual conversations? It makes sense that we talk about what we care about. The hope is that we are so deeply moved by and focused on the things of the Faith and the love of Jesus that we talk about them. The hope is that we discuss what the Word of God has been saying to us and we pray together and we set goals for ourselves and our family or community. In these conversations, we can plan together ways we can grow together in the Faith.

Understandably, conversations like this can be scary and difficult for many of us. There's a certain intimacy in our relationship with the Lord, and talking about it can make us feel very vulnerable. It's OK to recognize that but not to let it determine how we interact with one another. There's a great freedom, joy, and confidence—there's great fruitfulness—when we can bond with those we love on an intimate level and especially when that bond is sealed with the Holy Spirit as we talk about the Lord and what he is doing in our lives.

PRAYING TOGETHER

What can we do to allow the conversations to happen naturally, without being forced? A great practice is to have a small prayer together in the morning and at the end of the day. It's a way to share with one another the fact that God is the beginning and the end of all things, and so we give him the beginning and the end of our day. It just keeps us focused and keeps us rooted. Alluding back to the greenhouse image, our homes really are like the soil for our souls. There is no better way to keep our soil rich and fertile than by regularly watering it with family prayer.

SETTING GOALS TOGETHER

Another thing to do is to set goals together. Have a time each year when you set goals, personally or as a family or community, and then put them on paper. Again, this will look different for you depending on where you are in life, but I'll give some examples. You can apply them to your own journey.

One of these goals might be that you as a dad or mom will have a play date with your son or daughter at least once a month, maybe once a week, so you have an hour or two just to focus on and pour love into that particular son or daughter. This is a great opportunity as a parent to share your love for your children and the ways in which you're praying for them. It's a great opportunity to hear what's going on in their own lives.

Also, this is a great time for a husband and wife to commit to regular date times. With all of the needs and demands of life, especially if a family has multiple kids, it becomes very difficult for a husband and wife to set a time just to be together. But if you have a meeting to set goals, you can talk about the goal of committing to a regular date. You can talk about why you're doing it, so your children can hear and come to appreciate the importance of this time that you spend together. Then it will be much more likely that you'll be able to do it. And that will feed a very healthy culture, which will nourish and protect the marriage and the children.

Living Together Liturgically

One other unique approach to creating a Catholic culture in your life is the idea of living liturgically. This means allowing our faith—the seasons of the Church and the different feast days that we celebrate—to give purpose and direction to our daily lives.

There's no question that the proliferation of entertainment in our world is primarily the fruit of a loss of purpose or meaning. Where there is no understanding of a deeper mission to build up the kingdom of God, it's much easier for a faux purpose, an artificial purpose, to begin to take root. That artificial purpose bears fruit by making pleasure or entertainment the primary end of what we're doing. One way we are able to experience the medicine for this tendency and allow that medicine to bring healing to our minds and bodies is through a liturgical way of living.

FEAST DAYS

In the friary, we have the practice of not eating sweets or drinking festive drinks unless it's a feast day. If it's the feast of St. Francis, when you come down to the coffeepot at 5:30 in the morning, often you'll see right next to it a little box of donuts or some sort of sweet goody. This immediately communicates "Oh, it's a feast day," and it allows us to experience it corporeally, in our bodies—to "taste" and enjoy the feast day, which we're meant to do as human beings. It's the Catholic version of having a hot dog at the game. Catholic culture integrates a healthy humanity with a healthy spirituality.

In late winter at the friary, as Ash Wednesday approaches, all of a sudden we see the little snack cabinets empty out as those treats are given away in preparation for Lent. This communicates something to us, and it begins to prepare our hearts to enter into the Lenten season in a very human and natural and tangible way. So when the cookies come out for a feast day, we're not just eating cookies anymore, we're celebrating with the Church. Again, the meaning and purpose of the feast has worked its way into our world like leaven or like salt.

A beautiful aspect of allowing the liturgical calendar and the feast days to affect what we eat is that it fills even the small things of life with purpose and meaning.

I propose looking to the different saints of the day, especially in a family with children. One fun thing might be matching meals to the saint. For example, if it's the feast day of St. Thérèse, who is a French saint, maybe that's a great day to have French food. If it's St. Francis, an Italian saint, maybe that's the day you bring out the pasta. But the important thing is that the meal communicates and brings meaning. It makes the Faith something that deeply affects even the little things of our life. Those in our home are going to take notice, and it's going to bear fruit.

This would be a great opportunity then to catapult into a conversation. "Hey, we're having lasagna tonight because of the feast of St. Francis from Assisi. Do you know where Assisi is?" The feast and the food can guide the conversation and give it direction but also keep the conversation rooted in the Faith. Now understandably, this doesn't have to be something artificial or particularly pious—perhaps you want to have a conversation about Italy and you're going to talk about Italian cars or food or culture. But what's important is the meaning behind it. The reason for the conversation is it's the feast day of St. Francis.

Our faith bears fruit in the real stuff of our lives. As we continue the conversation about living liturgically, I'd like to offer some more suggestions.

THE CHURCH SEASONS

The Church gives us the liturgical seasons. The primary seasons I have in mind are the seasons of Advent, Christmas, Lent, and Easter. Is it possible for these seasons to really and truly affect us and bear fruit in our lives? Can our family life and our home take on a particular nuance that reflects these seasons? Perhaps some of the decorations in the house change.

Advent: Advent starts on the fourth Sunday before Christmas and marks the beginning of the Church year. It may be a fun idea to have a New Year's party that day celebrating the beginning of the new liturgical year. Advent calendars, even the cheesy ones, can be very helpful tools for initiating a daily conversation about the importance of Jesus' birth. Of course, it's always very fitting during the Advent season for a manger to be placed somewhere very conspicuous in the house. Can there be a time around the manger, maybe the morning and the evening prayer that we have together as a family?

Christmas: During Christmas, particularly the Christmas octave, we can celebrate together. Can we talk about the birth of Jesus and make sure that it is the focus of this season?

Many people don't know that Christmas is an octave; it's eight days. So, liturgically, we celebrate each day as if it is Christmas. Those eight days are a great time for a family vacation, if possible. We want to make sure we rejoice in each of those eight days. Why? To communicate and to experience this truth that Christmas is something that we celebrate and that we don't just celebrate for one day. We don't celebrate it as the world does. Let's take advantage of that. Imagine, especially if you have kids, the joy that they will have in knowing that they get to celebrate Christmas for eight days. It's a very positive, encouraging, and fruitful experience of the Church.

Lent: And of course, the season that we're all familiar with is the season of Lent. It's appropriate during Lent for our food to get a little bit simpler, our homes to get a little bit quieter, our screen time to be reduced. It's a great opportunity as Ash Wednesday approaches to have a conversation as a family: "What do we want to do as a family for Lent?" For the friars during Lent, we have a rule that makes it very specific that we fast during Lent.

But we also get together and have a conversation to say, "Well, is there anything extra we would like to do? Are there some prayers we'd like to add, a little extra penance we'd like to do?" Of course, what this will look like for a family won't be what it looks like for the friary. But nonetheless, it's a really great opportunity to have a very intentional, directional conversation that includes the Faith. It's a great time to hear from the children to allow them to take ownership of the Lenten season. It's a great time for them to hear Mom and Dad talk about it as well. Of course, we want to make sure that whatever we decide or discuss is balanced, but we do want to make sure that something is different. Lent needs to look different in our homes and hearts and lives than the Easter season or Ordinary Time looks.

Easter: The Easter season is fifty days. All fifty days should have a celebratory nature. The Easter octave is eight days, and we want to make sure we celebrate that well. The whole Easter season is a great time to have a few extra snacks around the house and to lighten up in a reasonable way some of the restrictions around sugar or around some forms of entertainment. It's a great opportunity to be more intentional about spending times of recreation together. Easter is another time that could be great for a family vacation.

We want to rejoice with the Church. God wants us to celebrate, and the Church invites us to celebrate in a special and very intentional way during the season of Easter. Like celebrating Christmas, it gives us a very positive incarnational and tangible experience of the Church and of the joy and the glory that is ours because of the Resurrection.

WEEKLY CYCLES

In a way, we can see two specific "seasons" in every week. In particular, I'd like to take a look at Fridays and Sundays.

Friday: We really do want Friday to have a different feel than the rest of the week. We don't celebrate Friday the way the rest of the world does. TGIF is not our slogan. Friday is not mainly the end of the work week and the beginning of the weekend. Friday is the day when we as Catholic Christians remember our Lord's passion and death. Fridays have a penitential nature for us. What that looks like is open to discernment. Historically it's been a common practice for Friday to be a day of abstinence. The mandatory nature of that has been nuanced, but the spirit behind it rings true and remains true.

We ought to take on some particular extra penance or prayer every Friday. It's a great day to schedule a holy hour, if that's possible. It's a great day to eat a simpler meal. It's a great day to dress more simply for work or for school. And if we do so, again, it allows us to experience the meaning of our lives. We can really drink deeply of the most beautiful gift that we have received, God's sacrificial death for us out of love for us and because of our sins. In short, it's an invitation to live more deeply as we experience more deeply the Lord's love and the beautiful meaning and truth of our lives. Friday points us to what is to come for us in the future.

Sunday: We absolutely must renew our celebration of Sundays. Sunday can't just be the day we go to Mass. Sunday is the day for family, a day to celebrate. Sunday is a day to have a special meal, to have a special time of recreation, to have special conversations. Sunday is a day for the family and for the Church, a day of rest and a day to celebrate.

Certainly it continues to make sense to get a little bit more dressed up for Mass. Again, this is a way to culturally experience and enter into and take ownership of the Faith. Sunday after Mass is also a great time to have a brunch, to go to the park, or to spend some time just being together. Now, we understand that life is complicated and messy and difficult, and sometimes having a totally protected Sunday won't be possible, but it's important to try.

Not long ago, another priest and I were with a young couple and their young child, a family who are practicing the Faith. We were talking about what it was in our lives that really made us take ownership of our faith. And for all of us, it had to do with conversations about Mass on Sunday and then going to Mass. For me, the moment that stands out the most is when my family would go on vacation to Palm Springs. We would have a conversation about "OK, what time is Mass?" or "Where is the nearest church to our vacation spot?" That told me that Mass is not just something we do at home but that we go to Mass on Sundays no matter what. Mass is not just a matter of convenience or circumstance.

For the other people I was talking to, going to Mass, especially when there were obstacles, really helped them take ownership of their faith. What this says to me is that focusing on Sunday is important. If we want to do battle with the world and all that the world is going to do to try to take us or our families away from going to church for the long haul, a great way to counteract that proactively is by really focusing on taking back Sunday. Make sure Sunday has a privileged place in our week and is a matter of our conversation. It really does bear fruit, and it really does make a difference.

Sunday—the nature of Sunday as the day of rest and of prayer and of family—is a gift the Lord wants to give us. Let's receive that gift.

Take the Next Best Step

Now, I realize I just gave you a lot—and I do mean a lot—to consider in creating a Catholic culture in your life and home. Just remember that our spiritual life is a real journey. It's a pilgrimage. Like any journey, it's made *poco a poco*, little by little, step by step. No one is expecting you to implement all these ideas at once. Depending on where you are in your faith life and depending on what your community looks like, some of these ideas may make more sense to you than others. The most important thing is to take the next best step *for you and your family* to ensure that the things you do move you toward creating a loving Catholic culture.

QUESTIONS FOR REFLECTION

How deeply does my Catholic faith permeate my life?

Do I pray together with my family?

Do we set goals together?

What is one way we can start living our lives more liturgically?

CHAPTER FOUR

Simplicity: The Christian Call to Contentment

When you live in the South Bronx, you get stories you just can't make up.

A brother and I were walking through the Bronx when we heard, "Hold up!" As we turned around, we saw a twenty-something-year-old woman from the neighborhood running toward us. "Where'd you get that?" she asked, indicating our habit. "Well, we're Franciscans, kind of like monks, and one of our brothers makes them." She was disappointed. "So I can't get my man one?" she asked. She liked the style and wanted him to look like us. "Yeah, sorry, they're not for sale," we responded with grins on our faces as she walked away. And we've got a bunch of stories like it.

It appears that if you fall far enough behind the latest fads, eventually you end up in fashion again. Admittedly, the Franciscan habit isn't going to be hitting European runways (or South Bronx sidewalks) anytime soon, but in one way we are back to a Franciscan fad. Simplicity is back in style.

As we'll see, there are a number of movements in the culture that are pushing toward cutting back and clearing out. And there's something to this that we want to pay attention to and learn from. We also want to take it deeper. What we'll find and focus on is that human beings have limited resources. We have limited time, energy, mental space, and so forth. While there are a number of "natural" fruits of living simply, the most foundational fruit is the way in which it brings us into a deeper intimacy with Christ. My hope with this chapter is that we are reminded that there is a different kind of wealth. There is a pearl of great price that is worth all you've got: intimacy with the heart of God.

The Attraction of Simplicity

Why is this movement toward simplicity of life so widespread? You're probably aware of a few of the movements out there. One of them is minimalism, which has become popular with millennials. It's based on a desire to have only what you need and use in your house or work space. You stick to only what's absolutely necessary. The design, the whole look, is very clean and simple.

There's also the huge popularity of Marie Kondo, who has written books and appeared on TV telling people how to tidy up. Really, though, she's teaching people to take a look at their possessions and get rid of things. She walks them through a little practice to understand whether they really value or need each of their possessions, and then if they do not, she invites them to discard it.

Another example is the popularity of what some call the capsule wardrobe, where you pick, say, twenty-one pieces of clothing and wear only those twenty-one pieces of clothing for three months. I know a number of young college students who practice this during Lent. Again, there's this natural and widespread understanding that there's something attractive, something peace-giving and meaningful, in a simpler approach to life.

My working theory is that these movements are popular because of a growing awareness of the burden of *things*. Materialism pressures you to compete with others. It pressures you to be constantly working, making money, and spending money. It also adds anxiety each day as you figure out how you're going to present yourself to the world.

I think people are experiencing a bit of dissatisfaction with materialism and the rat race—the anxieties and the pressures to own certain things, look a certain way, and present a certain image.

Poverty, Contentment, and Peace

What is the remedy for this disease? I propose that an essential component of the remedy is learning to be content. The first time I ever heard about the friars was from somebody who had been working with them, and he referred to them as the poorest but happiest men he had ever met. I was intrigued, and a sincere, deep-down desire began to rise to the surface that said, "I want that, I believe that, I recognize that as true."

Part of the secret is that our vow of poverty, which the culture often sees as an obstacle to happiness, is in fact the very reason for our happiness.

The Christian call to contentment is different from a Franciscan vow of poverty, but they're rooted in similar virtues and truths. The constitutions of the Franciscan Friars of the Renewal state that the friars are to "be content with the minimum necessary and not the maximum allowed."[6] I propose that this is the secret of authentic contentment. It's the key to appreciating small things and to putting a limit on greed, on the gluttony of accumulation.

Before saying more, I think it is necessary to make a distinction. There are in fact people today, and millions of them, who have a reasonable discontentment. They really do not have enough. It makes sense to be discontent if you don't have adequate food, shelter, health care, and important things like that. The audience for this chapter is specifically those who can cover their basic needs but get caught up in always wanting more.

Contentment is the ability to say "OK, that's enough." It's the ability to appreciate and be satisfied with what we have been given. It comes from an authentic understanding of what we actually need and what the accumulation of goods can actually offer. In other words, often the answer to our discontentment is not more stuff.

The fact is that we can be content—we can be happy and at peace—with much less than we probably think. But it's important for us to take possession of this truth, because we live in a culture that preaches the opposite—that we need more and more to be happy. In that worldview, the need for more is rarely questioned. An underlying philosophy that helps drive consumerism is the lie that the remedy for what I struggle with within can come from without. It's a "soft idolatry." It doesn't say material goods are to be worshipped, but it does get awfully close.

We know that media and marketing are fueled by money, by sales. Advertising is everywhere, constantly encouraging discontent and dissatisfaction, constantly proposing new items that we need. A majority of advertisers are not really concerned about you and your happiness. They're concerned with the bottom line. It's a very real battle for your pocketbook. Although it may seem like strong language, experience does suggest that sales often ride the tails of lies. Advertisements are geared toward evoking false needs and responding with false solutions. Strategically, and quite successfully, they show and don't tell you that you "need" this or that. My brothers and sisters, you probably don't "need" much of what you're being sold on TV, radio, and the internet.

Human beings are, in fact, capable of living without much at all. While we often don't want to emphasize this truth, it is an important fact to acknowledge. Without the latest this or that, you'll be OK and probably even better off. Let's be good with learning to say, "No, thanks, I'm good."

I like to share a brief story about an experience I had in postulancy as I was just learning to be a friar. It was the first time I experienced living a very austere, simple, even poor way of life. Remember that I chose this life, and I was drawn particularly to the friars because of the authenticity of the material poverty they strive to live.

So I was looking in our common medicine cabinet, where we keep extra toothpaste, toothbrushes, soap, and things like that. I was browsing through everything the way I used to browse around my favorite stores in the mall. And I found myself wanting, really wanting, the fancier, newer toothbrush. It was so colorful and shiny! I wanted it! I had to have it!

Luckily, I wasn't friar-shopping alone. Grace kicked in, and I realized how ridiculous I was being. I'd given up everything to follow Christ, left material possessions behind because I knew they weren't the answer to the questions my heart was asking, but now I was greedy for a one-dollar toothbrush? I took a deep breath, looked at the toothbrush, and thought to myself, "I know it's a big risk, but I think I'll be OK without the new toothbrush." I closed the cabinet and walked away. And wouldn't you know, I was OK without it.

This moment affected me so much because it gave me a great insight into my human condition. If I don't choose to be content with what I have, I am going to trade my contentment—my peace—for very, very little. We do have to choose contentment, to intentionally allow our reason to speak to our juvenile passions with some tough love: "Quiet down. You don't need it. You'll be fine."

Whether we've got loads or little, we need the capacity to choose contentment.

I remember clear as day the moment this truth struck me. I grew up in a town called Anaheim Hills. There was a vast difference between the wealth of those on top of the hill and those at the bottom of the hill. But we often all went to the same schools and played on the same sports teams. You couldn't tell who lived on the top of the hill or the bottom of the hill based on their happiness and peace. Why not? The acquisition of stuff wasn't the determining factor. The quality of their relationships was. The day I connected these dots was the day I was convinced that my life had to be about more than just the pursuit of wealth.

Detachment

"Detachment" is a popular Catholic word, which often is used in a slightly impoverished way. The idea of detachment is quite popular with young Catholics as they get fired up about the Faith and read great spiritual writers who talk about it. They think of detachment as letting go of things, but that is only part of the story. Detachment is never just a letting go; it's letting go of lesser things so that we can attach ourselves to something better, to a higher good.

We want to detach from a disproportionate or disordered attraction to goods, not because those things are bad and not just because they can steal our peace but because they get in the way of something higher and more beautiful. In fact, it is in our growing attachment to a higher value and a higher good that we receive the grace to detach from things that we may not need and that may actually be harmful for us.

I'd like to look at the story of the rich young man in Mark's Gospel. The young man comes to Jesus and asks the Lord what he needs to do to be perfect. The Lord tells him to observe the commandments. The young man says he has always done this. Then Jesus looks at him with love and says, "You lack one thing; go, sell what you have, and give to the poor … and come, follow me" (Mark 10:21).

The young man has great zeal. Jesus is inviting him to detach from his material possessions, to detach from self-reliance. And he's doing so by looking upon the young man with love. Jesus is inviting this man to receive the grace he needs by attaching himself to Jesus' look of love.

I cannot emphasize this enough. Jesus is inviting the young man to detach from what he knows by attaching himself to confidence and trust in the goodness of the one who invites him to something deeper, something more. We are not meant for a vacuum. We are not meant to detach for detachment's sake. Rather, we detach from material things by attaching ourselves to higher goods—ultimately, to the one alone who is good, our Lord Jesus Christ.

In other words, we always hold stuff with a light grip because we know it's not the answer to our deepest desires. Only Christ is. The stakes in acquiring the latest handbag, getting the promotion, having the perfect home aesthetic aren't intimately tied to our identity or sense of worth. When we're rooted in Christ's love and clothed with the dignity of our authentic identity, we're much freer to receive whatever God gives and to give whatever he takes.

The Desire for Peace and Freedom

So in these next few sections, we're going to look at what we want to be attaching ourselves to. The first area is the most universal and human and natural. We want peace and freedom. This is what the minimalistic movement and decluttering experts like Marie Kondo promise, which makes them so popular. They're tapping into this common, lived human experience and understanding that the accumulation of material possessions often robs us of peace and freedom.

QUESTIONS FOR REFLECTION

Do I feel pressure to wear certain name brands? Do I feel pressure to make a certain amount of money, to live in a certain neighborhood, to have a certain zip code because of what others will think?

Do I feel an internal pressure and internal desire to own certain things, which pushes me and drives me and compromises my peace?

Am I burdened with a heavy mortgage or bills? Am I living with constant financial anxiety that could be remedied by a simpler way of life and more frugal habits?

Now, I want you to imagine being content. Imagine no longer feeling so tied to the things that are stealing your peace, that deep down you know you don't need. Let your desire for enduring peace and freedom take precedence over the immediate gratification a quick purchase may propose. As Christians, we're not going to make our decisions from this place only, but we do want to pay attention to these competing desires.

A simpler life does have a cost. You may not get the same acclaim or attention from your neighbors. You may have to give up some of the pleasures or comforts that you've gotten used to. But you will have greater peace and greater freedom.

The Desire for Meaning

Before we talk about meaning, let's talk about clothes. I remember one time when I was in my twenties, I went out to buy a pair of designer jeans. I didn't have a ton of money, and I liked shopping, so I wanted to make just the right purchase. And I literally spent three hours in the mall just looking for jeans. When I found the ones I wanted, they were a proper name brand, and they looked good, and they fit right. And after that, when I wore them, I received a lot of compliments on them.

I really liked those jeans. There was something about them, about the name brand (and I've always been about name brands), that made me feel good and gave me some confidence. They gave me a feeling of value, a certain look, a certain appeal. And I liked that.

But there's a deeper meaning that gives an even greater joy, a greater peace. There are some ordinary things that are much more valuable than material riches, name brands, diamonds, German sports cars, white picket fences, and things like that.

When I went to World Youth Day in 2016, I was traveling to Poland with a group of twenty young adults, and I had with me a simple gray hat. It was totally plain, probably a five-dollar hat. As you might have guessed, I'm a bit of a style guy, or I *was* a bit of a style guy, and I thought, "Man, this is just too much gray." Plain gray on plain gray on plain gray. So what I did is, I had all the people I was traveling with sign their names on that hat with colored markers.

And now, half a decade later, it's still my absolute favorite hat. It's the best hat I've ever had because it means something to me, because all over it are the names of all these people. And with their names are the memories of what we did and of their stories, who they are. The names of these people on my hat have given it more value than any name brand I ever wore.

Now let's take a look at the Franciscan habit. Our habit is a long gray tunic adorned with a large hood, rope belt, and wooden rosary. As previously mentioned, it's not a style that's going to be the fad on European runways anytime soon, but I love it! It's a sign to me of my total consecration to Christ. It reminds me that he has chosen me to belong uniquely to him. Also, it's an incredible sign to others. Often when people refer to our habit, they tell us that seeing us wear it out in public gives them hope. My outfits no longer impress, but they do inspire.

I'm content with wearing the same habit every day because its purpose satisfies. It is enough for me. I'm happy wearing the same habit for years because it has meaning. Christian contentment is possible when we're not only satisfied with less but possess a less that means more.

Love for the Poor

We need freedom from luxury items and name brands for another reason as well. As we will discuss in detail in the next chapter, each of us as a Christian has a duty to be concerned with those who suffer and those who are poor. One way we can distance ourselves from the rat race of accumulating material possessions is by loving the poor.

There's a value in solidarity, in understanding that many people suffer greatly because of material poverty. We don't want to be tone-deaf or ignorant of that fact. It is healthy and holy to have a certain simplicity of life fueled by solidarity with the poor.

One simple way we can support the poor is to be mindful of our spending. If we are open to spending less money and buying less expensive things, we can set some money aside to put at the service of the Church and especially of the poor, who are dependent on our generosity.

There's a saying that we must live simply so that others may simply live. While I don't know who actually said that, there's something authentic about the statement. We need to hear the cry of the poor. We want to be proactive in our love and our care for them. And part of that means cutting back on excessive or unnecessary spending so we can show our love for our brothers and sisters who are dependent on our generosity.

God loves joyful givers, but also giving gives joy. Remember, my first introduction to the friars was as "the poorest but happiest men

I know." And I suspect the more you learn to say no to your little wants so you can say yes to another's enduring needs, the more you'll experience a lasting peace and overflowing joy.

Attachment to Jesus

So we see lots of reasons for simplifying our lives and detaching ourselves from the hamster wheel of materialism. But the little reasons serve the one big one, the real reason this matters. Like the rich young man, we are invited to follow Jesus. We're invited to be with him as he is present in our neighbors and in the poor. (He said, "As you did it to one of the least of these my brethren, *you did it to me*"—Matthew 25:40.) We're invited to be with him as he is present in the deeper intimacy of prayer, made possible by the peace and the freedom of a simpler life. We can live a simplicity the world doesn't value because we have a wealth the world doesn't know—the fullness received through intimacy with the Lord.

Remember that it was on the top of Mount Tabor, away from the common comforts and challenges of everyday life, that Jesus was transfigured, revealing his glory to his apostles. There's something in that for us. If we want to truly see the beauty of God, if we want to fall deeply in love with him in a way that is intimate and profound and fulfilling, it will be in part the fruit of a simpler way of life. It will be in part the fruit of a life attached to eternal realities and detached from the passing things of this life.

Again, we only have so much energy. If we spend our energy running after created goods, we may be too worn out to walk daily with our Creator. It's true! If we are running after less, we'll have more time to sit at the feet of Jesus in prayer, in reading and study, and in community—to hear his voice and see his most beautiful face. Think of Martha and Mary. Martha was distracted by so much, while Mary chose the better part by "wasting" time with the Lord.

That's why I think it is important that this chapter has a place in this book. You, the reader, are probably not called to take a vow of poverty like the Franciscans, but you are most certainly called to intimacy with God. My hope for you is that by learning to say "OK, that's enough" in regard to material possessions, you'll be free and more focused on your relationships, especially your relationship with Jesus.

Practical Tips

I want to be extremely practical now, because our reality is the lived experience of being in the world but not of the world.

BE CAREFUL ABOUT WHAT YOU LOOK AT

We are constantly being sold something. What I mean is that the world around us is always stirring up desires and making us doubt ourselves because of things we don't have. That's the way things get marketed and sold.

The desire for things wells up and grows in us mostly through what we allow in. The first thing to do if we want to get free of the constant need for more—the feeling that we don't have enough—is to be very careful about what we look at.

Often we're looking at what our neighbor or coworker is wearing. We're looking at the ring on his finger, the car he drives, and the house he lives in. We're looking at her Instagram or Facebook feed. All of this looking highlights a material possession, a thing, and it expresses something false. It says, "They have this diamond ring, so they must be happy." Don't compare and despair. It's a trap!

What I'm talking about is traditionally called custody of the eyes. In the realm of material possessions, it means you don't threaten your peace by looking at and scrolling through and fixating on the things that others have.

SHOP WITH A LIST

Second, when you are going shopping—at a grocery store or mall or online—go with a list. When you enter a store, you enter a place of marketing, where great minds have spent countless hours and millions of dollars thinking of ways to make you buy more than you thought you needed when you entered.

Remember: You're constantly being sold something, and the message under the sell is often untrue. So be intentional when you shop. Tell yourself, "This is the list of things I need. This is what I'm going to buy on Amazon." If, while you're online or at the store, some other item seems like a good idea, my recommendation is that you save it or write it down; let the new excitement and the rush of desire lessen a bit. Take an hour, a day, or a week and then revisit the item. See if you still find it good and helpful and necessary or if you can be content without it.

MAKE A BUDGET

It's prudent to have a very clear budget as a family. If you don't already, I'd recommend making one every year. Think about what you need, what is extra, and what you can set aside for the poor or another work of charity. I have heard of this practice among several Catholic families, some of them very wealthy. They set a budget for themselves, and they stick to it quite strictly. The foundational principle for the budget is what they actually need and not how much they can possibly spend. Then they make sure their surplus resources get directed to the poor and to works of the Church. In doing so, not only are they content on earth but also they are storing up treasures in heaven.

DO A CONTENTMENT CHECK

The friars have a custom four times a year, a quarterly poverty check. It's both personal and communal. We get out a sheet and take a look at our accumulation of goods. Do we have things that are unnecessary? Things we're not using? Things we can give away to the poor because others could use them better?

The practice of poverty checks comes from understanding the natural human inclination to accumulate; the things we have need to be regularly pruned. You might think of it as a quarterly contentment check or simplicity-of-life check instead. Whatever you call it, it's an opportunity for you personally or with your family to see how you're doing. You want to see if you have more than you need or if you have things that others need more. You look for things you can give away or put at the service of the Church. You also look for things that are making you like Martha, anxious about many things, instead of Mary, who chose the one thing necessary, remaining in Jesus' presence.

In closing, one final reminder: God is not outdone in generosity. If we sacrifice some of the pleasures that goods can offer for a greater ability to love him and be loved by him, especially through prayer, we'll truly come to rethink wealth.

QUESTIONS FOR REFLECTION

See "Contentment Check for the Laity" in the appendix.

CHAPTER FIVE

Love for the Poor:
Christ Knocks at Your Door

I'd like to begin with a quick reflection on three privileged places in the friars' encounter with God: the wood of the altar, the wood of the dining table, and the wood of the front door. In each of our friary chapels is erected a simple wooden altar around which we celebrate the Holy Sacrifice of the Mass each morning. At this humble wooden altar, we encounter the sublime humility of God every day. Around our dining table or, as we call it, our refectory table, we share each of our meals in common. Like the altar, it is made of unadorned wood. It is here each day that we encounter the good God through the goodness of the brothers. Finally, there is our front door. It is there that we have the privilege of encountering Christ in the distressing disguise of the poor: "As you did it to one of the least of these my brethren, *you did it to me*" (Matthew 25:40, emphasis added).

Back in 1987, when the Franciscan Friars of the Renewal were founded, a principle conviction that our founders legislated was that the friars would always live in neighborhoods noted for material poverty. In fact, it is stated that if the neighborhood ceases to be "noted for poverty," we will seek out a new residence.[7] There are many reasons why this value is dear to our hearts and our mission. One is that we want to be close to the poor so that they can always just walk over and knock on our door or ring the bell. We want to be physically and literally accessible to those in most need, and we're here in the name of Jesus and his Church. And we hold it to be a really privileged grace and invitation from the Lord to be this close to those who are so close to his own heart. We want to make sure a day doesn't go by that we can't have an encounter with Christ in the distressing disguise of the poor, just as we'd never go a day without encountering Christ around the altar in the Blessed Sacrament or around the table in community.

In a unique way, though, the Friars of the Renewal also feel that we're called to be a bridge between those who are most in need and the rest of the body of the Church. And so, in many ways, this chapter is me knocking on your door on behalf of those who knock on our doors. This chapter is my attempt to bring the poor to you—right to your door, right into your homes—and to remind all of us how intrinsically a part of our mission and the nature of the Church it is to love and serve the poor.

God's Mission and Our Participation

Let's go back for a moment and look at the foundation for the Church's mission to serve the poor. From the very beginning of the creation of man, God has always willed that man participate in his work. In the Garden, we have Adam being called to name the animals and till and keep the land. Later we have God asking Noah to build an ark and asking Moses to lead the Israelites out of slavery into the Promised Land. And it continues on into the New Testament. We have Our Lady's yes to the archangel Gabriel at the Annunciation as she participates, by her fiat, in the incarnation of the second Person of the Most Holy Trinity.

We see this continuing with the Church as Jesus sends out the disciples and sends out the apostles to baptize all nations in the name of the Father and of the Son and of the Holy Spirit. He sends them to continue his work, particularly through priests administering the sacraments. In a very real way, God freely has made us necessary participants in his mission. Without a doubt, he does the heavy lifting, but he does wait for our yes. He also allows us to say no.

And this includes the mission to love and care for those who are most vulnerable, most poor, most in need of help. It is an essential and central part of the heart of Jesus' mission to be near to those who are most in need. It is essential to serve and care for the poor. But, as has been the case throughout salvation history, God wants to work through us. So if Christians are not responding to the promptings of the Holy Spirit and the cry of the poor, everything's not going to be OK. If we respond to the promptings of the Holy Spirit and the cry of the poor with a no, people are going to continue to suffer. Therefore, we have a real responsibility and a real duty to respond to the promptings and the working of the Holy Spirit in our hearts and lives in a way that is proactive and even sacrificial.

Love for the Poor Reveals the Father

Explicitly through the Old Testament and implicitly through the life of Jesus, we are told again and again that God is a Father who hears the cry of the poor. And it's true. We can even say, in a special way, that those who are most in need are most near and dear to his heart. He has a special eye on them. It's also true, though, that those in need are at risk of not encountering the truth of God. They are at risk of not experiencing him as a Father who hears their cry if Christians themselves, Christ's mystical body, do not hear and respond to that cry. And while the main thrust of this chapter is going to be serving and caring for the material needs of the poor, it's important at the very beginning to found the Church's mission on Jesus' own mission of revealing the identity of the Father.

Through his work and through his words, Jesus reveals the nature of God, the truth of God, which is salvific. The mission of Jesus has been given to us: "As the Father has sent me, even so I send you" (John 20:21). At the heart of our service to the poor, we also have the call to reveal to the world the truth about the nature of God, that God is alive, that God is good, that God is Father, and that God truly hears the cry of the poor.

If Christians are not loving the poor, it's not surprising that the rest of the world has doubts about the existence of God or the nature of God.

One of my absolute favorite stories is the story of a man—we'll call him Nick—who showed up on the doorstep of our shelter in the South Bronx on his first night out of prison in many years. Life had not been easy on him. You could tell that he had a trying background and struggled with authority and had a hard time getting along with others.

Like any shelter, ours has a certain structure and requires a certain degree of discipline and following of rules. And for weeks and months, you could see Nick struggling with it. He was one of the guys who required a little more attention, a little more talking to, and to be honest, he was just an all-around rough character.

And then Nick's birthday arrived. At the shelter, we take note of the birthdays of all of the men who come, and then on that night we celebrate them. So in keeping with this tradition, we had a cake made with Nick's name on it and we stuck some candles in it. Toward the end of our communal dinner that evening, we turned off the lights and brought out the lit cake, and all the men in the shelter and our missionaries and the friars sang "Happy Birthday." As we put the cake down on the table in front of Nick, he looked at it and he immediately began to sob, the tears just pouring out. When our "Happy Birthday" song ended and all eyes were on Nick, you could hear him whisper, shaking his head, "I've never had a cake with my name on it before. I've just never had a cake with my name on it before."

Nick had a rough life. He had a broken family, and he never experienced the unique love he deserved. He never experienced a love that was just for him, that knew his name and celebrated him. Could we really expect Nick to have faith in a God who is a Father—who loves him and knows him and rejoices in him uniquely, who has created this world in many ways uniquely for him as a gift, just for him with his name on it—if he hasn't experienced this through the community, through the Church, through family?

And so, in this little way of receiving a personalized cake and hearing "Happy Birthday" sung just for him, he became open to the possibility that God also loved him and cared for him and knew his name. Over the remaining time that Nick stayed with us, the truth is he was never the same. He softened. He was tender. Simply by being open to being loved, he was given a new heart and a new outlook on life.

And this is our work as a Church—through our acts of charity, giving people an experience of the authentic love that God has for them.

An "Eighth Sacrament"

There's nothing more beautiful or more filled with joy and peace and light than a life of service to the poor. It's a life filled with mission and purpose. It's a front-row seat to the work of God. Working with the poor gives us insight into our own hearts as we discover that we are able to love sacrificially. And if you struggle with self-doubt, there's no greater remedy than loving others sacrificially and being able to recognize in yourself the depth of your character and potential. There's also nothing that gives us a more profound insight into the very heart of God than when we love as Jesus did.

In many ways, Jesus wants to teach us using the Montessori method, giving us chances to get our hands dirty. He wants to teach us in the activity of our daily lives. As we are meeting people in need and hearing their stories, learning their names and pouring ourselves out and serving them, we are being given a chance to love them the very way that God loves us.

As you serve others, you're also loved by them. If you want to experience love, there's a great and privileged place to love and be loved in work with the poor.

We know that the poor are to be loved because they deserve to be loved. We don't do this because of some ulterior motive. People are ends in themselves. But at the same time, it's worth noting that there are benefits. There are fruits. There are real gifts that come from our service to the poor.

Fr. Benedict Groeschel, one of our founders, often spoke of the poor somewhat poetically as the "eighth sacrament." This is why. Jesus said that what you do for the least of his brethren, you do for him. And so in a very real way, as we love the poor, we encounter Jesus in them. I'll even dare to say this: If our encounter with Jesus does not include an encounter with him in the poor, our encounter with Christ is incomplete. There's a part of the radiant face of Christ that is still in shadows.

What's the Next Best Step?

The reality is, a life of service to the Church and to the poor is a life of great joy and great happiness. I will focus on that, but at the same time, it's important not to forget what's at stake. There's a phrase popular today about being tone-deaf, and often celebrities or public personalities are accused of this. Being tone-deaf is when you're speaking in a way that seems out of touch with a deeper reality. Generally, it is making light of or speaking flippantly of a situation that actually is very severe and causing suffering for a lot of people.

One of my fears for many Christians today is that they're accidentally living tone-deaf lives, even in some of the most beautiful works and ministries of the Church. So the question is simply this: Are our lives rooted in reality? Are they consistent with following a loving God, a God who calls himself Father? Are they consistent with the suffering of our brothers and sisters throughout the world?

I don't think it's necessary at this point to go into the numbers around poverty, homelessness, addiction, or children being raised as orphans without parents. I think we are in touch with that reality, at least on an abstract, theoretical, and technical level.

Instead, let's just take a moment and look at our own lives. Let's take a moment and look at the things that we think about, stress out about, and spend our money on. If we were to invite a person who is living as a refugee or if we were to invite a mother who is struggling to feed her four or five kids on her own and doesn't know where tonight's meal is going to come from—if we invited that mother into our head, or into our home, could we do so with a clear conscience? Or would we be embarrassed by what she saw? The important thing to remember is this is not a time for an accusation or condemnation. It's the effect of a culture we live in, and in many ways, we are passive recipients of our culture and our worldview.

The step that I would like to encourage at this moment is just an honest reflection and examination of conscience. If, in your heart, you know that you can do better—that you can live more in continuity with the cry of the poor, which continues day in and day out—can you prayerfully start to discern the next best step?

Obstacles to Loving the Poor

I'd like to take a look at some of the obstacles to loving the poor in the modern world, reasons we don't do it. We'll take a look at four different obstacles, which are probably the most common, especially among those who might be reading this book. The first is indifference. The second is making time. The third is judgment. And the fourth is not knowing a clear way to help or respond.

INDIFFERENCE

Indifference isn't a question of coldness so much as concreteness. For many of us, the poor are an abstract concept. We know of the poor, we know about orphans, we know about the abused in a theoretical sense, but we don't know their names and we don't know their stories. Because we don't know their names and their stories, our hearts are not moved to the degree they should be.

Let's look at the parable of the Good Samaritan (Luke 10:25-37). Before the Good Samaritan actually begins to help the man who was beaten up and left on the side of the road, the Scriptures say, he sees him and his heart is moved with compassion. For us to really and passionately begin this mission of going toward the suffering and proactively seeking them out, our hearts need to be moved with compassion. This grace is received through true encounters with the true suffering of our neighbors. While we can't synthetically manufacture these experiences, we can intentionally seek them out. If we want to love like the Good Samaritan, can we go in search of the lost like the Good Shepherd?

One striking moment like this happened to me when I was living in Honduras. It was my responsibility to help interview the mothers who were coming to request a little bit of food to help them get through the month. And the fact is that everyone who came was in need to some degree, but because our supplies were limited, we had to focus on those most in need.

I remember interviewing one of the mothers in Spanish. I asked her name, and she gave me her name. Then I asked her age, and she said, "I don't know." And I almost jokingly responded, "You don't? You don't know?" "No, no, I don't know." And she pulled out of her pocket a government-issued ID to show me. I said, "OK, well, what does it say on there?" And she looked at me, and she said, "I'm sorry, I can't read." She handed me the license, and I looked at it and did the math. I told her how old she was and her birthday. She was in her twenties.

At that time, I was twenty-seven years old. Growing up, there was no doubt or question for me about going to a university. It was just a question of which one. And there was no doubt or question about what job I would have or what kind of home I would be able to buy. It was just expected. And here I was, interviewing a woman who was in many ways a peer of mine, and she couldn't read. For me, this was one of those moments of really coming into contact with the effects of poverty and how different the life experience of many people in the world is from mine. This woman's name, her face, and her story continue to move me to love the poor with more fervor.

An aspect of this interviewing process was going out and visiting homes, basically to corroborate the women's stories. We went to one mountain village in Honduras and came to a house where a twelve-year-old girl was living with her grandparent. As she was showing me the one-bedroom hut with a dirt floor that we would hardly call a house, I asked her, "OK. So what's for dinner tonight?" And she said, "I don't know." I thought maybe she was kind of joking—maybe she was playing up the poverty to make sure that we helped her—so I immediately responded, "What do you mean you don't know?" And she looked at me sincerely and said, "We don't have any food, so I don't know what we're going to have for dinner." When I feel inclined to pettiness or to turning in on myself, this girl's name, her face, and her story root me back in reality.

The suffering of the poor is not abstract. The effects of a widespread indifference or unawareness of the cry of the poor are not abstract. *Lord, help us to see what you see and feel what you feel.*

QUESTIONS FOR REFLECTION

Is part of my heart not moved because I don't have names and faces and stories to connect with, or to pierce through, the abstraction?

Is there a way for me to discerningly seek to learn some of these stories and some of these names so that my heart might truly be moved, as the heart of Jesus was, as the heart of the good Samaritan was?

LACK OF TIME

A second real obstacle is quite simply the question of time. Our time is very limited and is given over to many tasks, many of them important ones. To say this simply, you have to make time for the poor. It's probably going to be sacrificial, and that's OK. You and I have been the recipients of a sacrificial love through the love of Jesus, and you and I are called to live and love as Jesus did. And the fact that something is difficult does not excuse us from the call to do it—to love the poor, to accept a radical mission to those in need. God's healing isn't going to happen without our free and very intentional choice.

In the Gospel of Matthew, chapter 19, Jesus reminds us that those who have given up lands or brothers or sisters or mother or anything for his name will be repaid a hundredfold. This repayment is not a literal transaction, like I sacrifice one cow and God gives me a hundred. Often it's something deeper. What God is saying to us is that he's inviting us to sacrifice for those in need, and he will repay that sacrifice a hundredfold in the temporal world but also in the eternal. It's never too late to start storing up treasures in heaven!

As mentioned in our chapter on prayer, time wasted on the Lord is never time wasted. Likewise, time spent serving the poor, in obedience to the call of the gospel, is always time well spent. Remember, we have a God who loves us with a hundredfold love. These times of service will absolutely enrich our entire lives, but they will also enrich our entire eternal lives. Don't hesitate to allow the rewards of eternity to inspire you to love now with more urgency.

Now I'd like to come at a similar truth but from a different angle. In Matthew 25, when Jesus talks about judgment in this iconic passage, the judgment is this: Those who will go to the reward of eternal life are those who fed Jesus when he was hungry, gave him something to drink when he was thirsty, visited him when he was in prison, and gave him clothes when he was naked. And those who will be condemned are those who committed sins of omission: They didn't feed the hungry, clothe the naked, or visit the imprisoned. Not using your time to perform works of mercy in this time will also have eternal consequences. I hope to remind you of this gently but authentically: sins of omission will be judged. With God's help, let us make the time to love the poor. Our salvation depends on it.

QUESTION FOR REFLECTION

When I place myself prayerfully in the scene painted in Matthew 25, am I grouped with those who "did it to me" by serving the hungry, thirsty, naked, etc., or with the group who did not?

PASSING JUDGMENT

A third obstacle, which we'll touch on briefly, is judgment. It's a common thing. For example, perhaps the people in the shelter have a struggle with addiction or perhaps they've come to our country from another country. A common excuse for not helping these people is to say, "Well, they shouldn't have used drugs or alcohol" or "They should have stayed in their own country." We could go into all of the details about the factors that might have led some people to make those decisions, even factors that reduced their culpability because of the homes they grew up in. But without going into those details, the shortest and most poignant answer is quite simply this: you and I have a savior.

You and I have been loved with a love of mercy. That love has come down to us and picked us up and pulled us out of the difficulties, the destruction, the chains with which we have chained ourselves by our own sins. You and I are the recipients of a merciful love and not a condemning love. And Jesus said, "As the Father has sent me, even so I send you" (John 20:21). You and I, out of gratitude for this sacrificial and merciful love that we have received, are called to love likewise. At a certain point, there is room for justice. No question about that. But we can't just dismiss people because they are in bad situations that they caused for themselves. If somebody is in distress, we come to their help. That's what the Church does because that's what Jesus does.

QUESTIONS FOR REFLECTION

How deeply do I live from the truth that I have been loved with a merciful love, a saving love?

Does this draw my heart to love likewise, or do I hesitate to love others because they "don't deserve it"?

NOT KNOWING HOW TO HELP

The last difficulty is not knowing what to do. How do I help? What does help actually look like? Often our hearts are moved, and in the moment we know we want to help. We want to do something, to respond to the cry of the poor—maybe even in a radical way. But how? If we don't find a very clear and immediate answer, we end up getting distracted, or we start giving our time and energies to other things that are a little bit more accessible.

For the moment, I'm just going to talk about the principle; we'll get into the concrete at the end of the chapter. The point I want to make here is about the creativity of love. When you love someone, you find ways to be with that person. You create ways to serve that person. So my invitation to you is to prayerfully reflect on this.

QUESTION FOR REFLECTION

What are ways my gifts can serve the poor, ways my talents and resources can be given to the poor? Brainstorm some suggestions. The idea is to carve out some time to pray and some time to research and ask questions, doing a little bit of proactive work so that I can respond wholeheartedly to the poor.

Witnesses: It Is Possible

Love is creative, and this is what you and I are called to. Each of us has our own way of loving creatively. Here are some examples: One of the friars' friends is a retired nurse. We'll call her Patsy. For over twenty-five years, including while she was working full-time, Patsy has come and cooked dinner at our homeless shelter. Also, as a nurse, she has participated in multiple international medical brigades, where she's put her professional skills to use offering life-saving, life-changing surgeries and medical care to those in most need. Patsy could have spent her Tuesday evenings for the past twenty-five years very differently, but she chose to sacrifice them—"make them holy"—by dedicating them to the poor. She'll be the first person to tell you that she acts out of love. Remember that hundredfold promise? Patsy is living proof.

Another is Charlie Moran, a florist on Long Island who has been feeding the friars in the New York area for some twenty years. Charlie heard about the needs of the friars and began a group called Friar Suppliers. He got a network of families together from his church and his rosary group and other places. And now for decades, they've been raising money to help provide groceries to multiple friaries and convents every month. His understanding is that he is feeding those who feed the poor, and by helping us he's helping those most in need at our shelter. Charlie's service to the poor has come at a great cost and countless hours, but the Father is never outdone in generosity. Charlie Moran is a husband, father, florist, faithful disciple of Christ, and lover of the poor.

Finally, I'll share a larger-scale example of what service to the poor looks like. One of my favorite charities is Mary's Meals. The story of Mary's Meals is miraculous, heroic, and incredibly beautiful. It was started by two brothers in Scotland in the 1990s. They wanted to help with relief efforts during the Bosnian war, so they collected a load of food, clothing, and medicine from the people in their town, took a few days off from their jobs, and drove to Bosnia as part of an aid effort. When they got back home, they were surprised that people kept sending aid. By 2019, it had reached a point where they were feeding more than 1.5 million children around the world. They feed them at the children's schools. And they're able to feed each child for a whole school year for just twenty-one dollars.[8]

Loving the poor: It is possible. It is necessary. It is beautiful. It reveals the Father to the world, and it reveals the Father to us.

QUESTIONS FOR REFLECTION

Are there any charities close to my heart that serve the poor?

If I do not know of any, do I have any friends who currently serve in my community that I can reach out to?

Can I ask my parish for ways I can donate my time or money to serve the poor?

What areas of spending might I be able to cut down on to put some money aside for those in need? And if not financially, in what ways can I carve out time to help those in need?

CHAPTER SIX

Priests by Baptism: "Christian, Remember Your Dignity"

It's 4:45 a.m., Harlem, New York. Slowly but surely a half dozen barefoot friars quietly enter the chapel. Candles are lit. A hymn is intoned, and Jesus in the Most Blessed Sacrament is taken from the tabernacle and enthroned on the altar, where he'll be adored for the next hour.

The first obligatory prayers in the friary aren't until 6:00 a.m., but during peak COVID, quarantine, and social unrest, the friars of St. Joseph Friary decided that, as a sacrifice, each morning they would make a holy hour interceding for the world. It's a practice they've chosen to extend indefinitely. There's a beauty to it that is immediately obvious, but there's also a potency to it which we'll use this chapter to take a look at.

"Christian, remember your dignity."[9]

Powerful words. These words are taken from a sermon by St. Leo the Great that we read each Christmas morning as we recite the Liturgy of the Hours. Christian, remember your dignity. Remember who you are and what you are capable of.

These next three chapters could be called a "remembrance of our Christian dignity." We'll take a look at what it means to be baptized into the life and mission of Christ, specifically his roles as Priest, Prophet, and King.

We are not powerless. Christian, remember your dignity.

The greatest force in history is prayer united with sacrifice. Dear Christian, by your Baptism you have access to power as a member of the priesthood of the baptized. Christian, remember your dignity.

There's a whole lot of good news in these words, and they're a great reminder of the capacity and responsibility that we share as members of the baptismal priesthood. When we look at our world today, it's very easy to feel powerless and give in to discouragement or despair. The platforms of many people in media, politics, and other influential positions often promote a worldview with morality and ethics contrary to the gospel. Those of you with children may feel afraid and can struggle with the question, What can I do? How can I protect my children? How can I live the gospel in a world where it feels like there's not just one Goliath, but many Goliaths?

Like David, we can have confidence in knowing we're not in this fight alone. The Lord is with us, and he has given us our own little slingshot and pebbles: prayer and sacrifice. I believe it's also important to note that we're not only trying to survive. We're not only trying to get by. We're not only trying to minimize our wounds. Instead, we're trying to build the kingdom of God. Like David, we're fighting to win. And with God's help it is indeed possible.

We're not just trying to slide into heaven or sneak our way into the pearly gates. We're trying to bring renewal and growth and new life into our families, our communities, our Church, and our world. It is possible, my brothers and sisters. And a key element to reclaiming the world for Christ is going to be reclaiming and living from the identity that comes from our baptismal priesthood.

Prayer and Sacrifice

In Romans 12:1, St. Paul writes, "I appeal to you therefore, brethren, by the mercies of God, to present your bodies as a living sacrifice, holy and acceptable to God, which is your spiritual worship."

Let's talk about what our spiritual worship looks like. I'd like to start by using the image of the offering of incense, which is a perennial image of offering prayers to God. The Church Fathers throughout history have viewed the offering of incense this way. There is the hot coal, and then there's the incense. And you need both. Because it's not until the incense touches the hot coal that the incense burns and its aroma starts to fill the air. In a sense, the burning incense fills the world and rises up to the heavens.

As you need both coal and incense for the incense to rise, likewise we need both sacrifice and prayer in our role of the baptismal priesthood. Often, sacrifice is compared to the burning coal, and our prayers are like the incense. When we bring them together, we're united in the cross of Christ. And as we know, the prayer and the sacrifice of Christ were so powerful that they renewed and redeemed the whole world.

Remember that the work of Christians, of building the kingdom of God, is a collaboration between God and men. We have a part to play. And sometimes you might ask, "Why do we need to pray? Why do we need to offer intercession? Why do we need to make sacrifices? Isn't the sacrifice of Christ enough? Doesn't God already know our prayers and our needs before we speak them?" The answer in one sense is yes. But God invites us to participate in his work, as he has done throughout salvation history. He wants us to share in prayer and sacrifice, in the same prayer and sacrifice of Jesus.

In a certain sense, when we till the soil of the earth before we plant the seeds that grow, we are participating in God's feeding us. In a similar manner, in our prayer and our sacrifices, we are tilling the ground of the spiritual life. His grace, like rain, will fall, but if we have not prepared the soil through our prayers and sacrifices, it will lack fruitfulness.

To use another image, remember David. The victory was the Lord's, but David had to make himself available, pick the rocks, load the slingshot, and sling a rock at Goliath. Likewise in our world, the victory will be the Lord's, but we have a duty to make ourselves available, pick the rocks by making sacrifices, and throw the rocks by offering prayers.

This may sound heavy or intimidating, but it isn't really. It just means recognizing the sacrifices that you're already offering and being more intentional with them and with your prayers.

It's an invitation to take a look at our own lives and discipleship, to recognize the ways that our fidelity to Christ has already brought us into a place of offering continual sacrifices.

In our constitutions, the friars have a section on penances. One of the paragraphs, which is filled with a lot of wisdom, talks about how the friars are to accept the daily sufferings and burdens of their life—for example, the tiredness, the traffic, the noise, and all the different elements of living in the South Bronx, New York City. (Like finding parking on a Sunday night. The worst.) The friars are called to accept these and to offer them as penance, to offer these as sacrifices to the Lord.

In other words, it's a great gift to recognize the ways our daily actions can be sacrificial. Following Christ actually already involves picking up our crosses daily. We already have a coal that is burning. We already have the rocks to throw at Goliath in our daily lives. While we will discuss the possibility of adding sacrifices and how to discern those, for the time being, let's take a moment to recognize the many ways we are already making sacrifices for the Lord. Also, I'd recommend looking to grow in fidelity before taking on extra corporal penances. For example, I'd pursue greater patience, less gossip, more purity, reconciliation of relationships, and so forth before fasting more, sleeping less, and the like.

So what does this look like for a non-friar? Let's take as an example a great friend of mine who at one point in his life was discerning which way to go with his career. He had a chance to continue in marketing in Hollywood, making tons of money and driving European sports cars. But he decided instead that he wanted to give his life to the Church. He still has a good home, a good job, and all of that, but he doesn't have a Lamborghini. Now, in his everyday life, what God sees and God receives is that he doesn't have some of the luxuries, money, fame, or glitter that he could have had if he hadn't decided to dedicate himself to the service of the Church. And so each day, as he continues to be faithful to this offering, he can give this sacrifice to God.

Maybe you've had a moment at work where you could have acted in a way that was cutthroat, stepping on someone else to get ahead, and you chose not to do that. And so maybe you didn't get a promotion. And without that promotion, you didn't get a little bit more authority, a little bit more vacation time, and a little bit more money to spend. Your fidelity to that choice is something you can give to Jesus.

I also think of those of you who are mothers or fathers. Raising your children is a work in the kingdom of God. You've been open to life, and as you have given yourself to serving your kids—waking up in the middle of the night to feed them as babies, struggling to help guide them as they become teenagers—you suffer with them. You work in the workplace to make money to provide for them, to help them get a good education, to allow them to go on mission trips or partake in different activities for their own growth. All of this is building the kingdom of God, and all of these little sacrifices and labors make the coal burn. And as we pray, these are all beautiful things to offer to the Father. These are all ways we are already participating in our baptismal priesthood. All we have to do is recognize them and actually offer them to Jesus.

As we recognize and come to value and appreciate these little offerings we make in the name of Jesus, it gives us the meaning and the dignity of our lives. It is an offering that renews the world and the Church and unleashes the most powerful force in human history—prayer united with sacrifice. But it also gives us grace and foresight when temptation comes. When the invitation comes to look after ourselves to get ahead, we know that we can be faithful to the gospel. We can be humble. We can be generous, and we can be sacrificial because we understand that we are living in the midst of a spiritual battle. We know that these offerings—these little sacrifices—are efficacious for the renewal of the Church, the renewal of the world, and the salvation of souls.

To help bring this home, consider a woman who lived this way: Mother Teresa. When something went wrong in her life, Mother Teresa had a beautiful attitude. When she missed out on good things because of her fidelity to Jesus, she knew these were little sacrifices. What Mother Teresa was able to see is that these little sacrifices were not just good things she missed out on but good things that were actually offered to God. While *Time* magazine may not have known to what level they were right when they named Mother Teresa one of the most powerful women in the world, they were on to something. Mother's influence on the world, one that continues to renew it today, is the fruit of her prayer and sacrifice.

QUESTIONS FOR REFLECTION

Can I take a moment and prayerfully reflect on ways in which I am already making regular sacrifices out of fidelity to Christ?

Can I ask for the gift of faith, so that the Holy Spirit can convict me anew of my dignity and capacity as a member of the priesthood of all the baptized?

Developing the Habit

Now I'd like to take a look at how we can actually begin to develop this habit and begin to see as Mother Teresa saw. If you remember, bread and wine are offered at the offertory of the Mass, and these are the gifts of the Church. As members of the baptismal priesthood, we bring these gifts. They are in the form of bread and wine, but they are representative of our entire selves. The bread and wine are the "work of human hands" that lie before the altar. The priest then receives these gifts of the baptized and places them on the altar. Through the prayers of consecration, they become the Body, Blood, Soul, and Divinity of Christ. These sacrifices of the Church are united to the offering of Jesus to the Father. They are returned to their source and reach their summit through the Holy Sacrifice of the Mass.

Now, what does this mean for you? Christian, remember your dignity. Each and every sacrifice you make throughout your day can be "placed on the altar." All of it can be returned to God during Mass and united to the offering of Christ to the Father. In other words, your little fidelities are united with the greatest prayer and sacrifice of all time, the sacrifice of Calvary. You are not powerless.

The offering at Mass is not a time to check out and just wait for the next response. Instead, it's a great time for us to interiorize and to call to mind those little sacrifices that we have been making throughout the week. It's a time to place them on the altar to unite them with the sacrifice of Jesus. It works if you work it.

How do we facilitate this? How do we pay attention to this? I would recommend making it part of your daily regular examen to recognize the ways you are making sacrifices day in and day out for the Lord. Especially if you have kids, you can ask them at the end of the day, "OK, can you think of one or two things that you did today that you offered to God?"

Perhaps you have a child in elementary school, and somebody said something mean to her. As you talk with her about her experience, you learn that she didn't say something mean back because she knows it's not what Jesus would want her to do. And that would be something that she could take note of. Then on Sunday, before Mass or during the offertory, you can help your child to place that on the altar: "Remember that little sacrifice of not returning an insult for an insult? We can give that to Jesus to make him happy."

What we're doing is recognizing what we're already doing. But we're also forming a worldview and forming our sons and daughters in their dignity in the baptismal priesthood. You know, all priests go to seminary. They're taught how to offer sacrifice. And in the domestic church, in our homes, it's up to the parents to mentor their children in their role as members of the baptismal priesthood.

I encourage you to invite the Holy Spirit to reveal to you the daily sacrifices you're already making, the daily struggles that you're enduring because of your fidelity to Jesus. And we want to orient these toward the Holy Eucharist, the source and summit of all things. Part of orienting our sacrifices toward the Eucharist is this ongoing reflection. We take note, very particularly, of these little sacrifices we're making. Then when we go to Mass on Sundays, or daily, we very intentionally give these gifts to Jesus as the bread and wine are placed on the altar during the Holy Sacrifice of the Mass.

Offering Jesus our daily sacrifices is part of our spiritual tradition. St. Thérèse of Lisieux talked about how, when she was a child, her family would have a manger set up in preparation for Christmas. As the children made a sacrifice, they could place a piece of straw in the manger to give a little something to comfort Jesus and to welcome him. Similarly, some people have a cord with ten beads in their pocket. The goal is to make sacrifices for Jesus throughout the day. As each sacrifice is made, a bead is moved from left to right until all ten beads have been moved. At night, these sacrifices are offered to Jesus, and in the morning you begin again.

You may have other ideas for doing this; you can be creative. But at the bottom of it, we just want to recognize what we're doing. We want to name it, to see that we're giving good gifts to God, and to be reminded of the great dignity we already have by the nature of our baptismal priesthood.

QUESTIONS FOR REFLECTION

Is there a way to pay attention to the sacrifices I'm making so that I can intentionally unite them with the offering of Jesus?

Can this practice be a source of motivation to choose the right action even when it's difficult?

Intercessory Prayer

As we know, love is not just about us. It's not just about making sure we're reminded of the great things that we're doing for Jesus. Instead, it's oriented toward others and toward building up the whole kingdom of God.

So here let's take a look at intercessory prayer. I've had a chance to work with a group of young men who are missionaries at our homeless shelter, and they're very zealous. During evening prayer each night, we have an opportunity to offer intercessory prayers, and it's like the Franciscan news feed. One of the missionaries will say, "I'd like to pray for Ramona. Ramona, I met her when I was on a walk today, and she has four children and sixteen grandchildren. And two of the grandchildren are preparing to take tests, and they're really nervous. And if they don't pass one more time, then they're not going to be able to become a certified dentist. And so Ramona is really worried about it. And on top of that, she has some difficulties with finances. Let us pray to the Lord." And they kind of really, really go into details.

And then, "I'd like to pray for Clarence. Clarence gave us a call, and Clarence, he's Nigerian, but he's been in the States for fourteen years. And he used to work as an engineer, but then he had a difficult time at his job. Plus, he's a Yankees fan, and they're on a losing streak. Let us pray to the Lord." And it's quite comical how detailed the missionaries get about these people they meet, the people who call, the checkout woman at the supermarket.

But it's also quite beautiful because what it's saying is that they're not just in the crowd. They're not just watching life, but they're deeply invested in it. They're paying attention to those they meet and taking their stories and their needs to heart.

It's a beautiful practice to cultivate for all of us as Christians. Without a doubt, we are all invited to be men and women of intercessory prayer. We're invited to pray to God on behalf of the whole world—to pray for the salvation of souls, to pray for an end of suffering, to pray for the needs of all our brothers and sisters. Certainly we're going to pray first for our family and friends and coworkers—those in our immediate circle. But can we also have a time, even each night, to offer intercession as a family for those we meet along the way?

One of the greatest and most beautiful gifts I've had as a friar is being invited to share in different families' times of prayer together. And it's somewhat common for a family with kids to get together at the end of the night to make the Sign of the Cross, to thank God, and then to have a time just to pray for others. They ask, "Who would you like to pray for?" And each of the children offers a prayer. It's incredibly beautiful and moving to me, but it also must be incredibly beautiful and moving to the Lord.

This practice of intercessory prayer is forming these children to pay attention to those they meet. It's forming them to have open hearts that are invested in their brothers and sisters they meet along the way. It makes sure that their interactions don't just become horizontal human interactions. Instead, they are learning to bring these prayers and these needs of their suffering or concerned neighbors and friends to the Lord.

This is part of that participation in the work of God. God wants to rain down his grace and healing power upon the world, but sometimes he needs us just to open that door, to pierce the heavens through our prayers. The fruitfulness will be his, but the key that unlocks the door has been given to us.

QUESTIONS FOR REFLECTION

Am I paying attention to the people I meet throughout the day?

Am I hearing their stories and allowing my heart to be moved by them?

If I don't already have the practice, can I begin interceding for those I meet throughout the day?

Intentions

Let's now take a look at how we can pray for particular intentions. While we're always invited to have hearts that are open to the whole world, nonetheless we're going to have a particular care for certain people entrusted to us. We're going to want to pray for these people. For example, we're going to pray for our children, our parents, our other family members, and our friends in a more intentional way that unifies prayer with sacrifice.

We want to make sure to unite these particular prayers for the needs and sufferings of our closest brothers and sisters with some sort of sacrifice. And that can take two forms.

The first form is something that I've been practicing now for years, and I'm really convinced of its fruitfulness. I'm convinced of the fruitfulness of a small and consistent sacrifice for a particular intention.

I had the opportunity to be the director of Catholic Underground for a number of years. And there was a period where every month, there was some drama. Every month, something went wrong and a problem had to be solved. I was open to the idea that perhaps there was a spiritual dynamic to all of this. And I felt prompted to do something quite simple. I said, "For the remainder of my time being the director of Catholic Underground, I'm not going to eat peanut butter."

Peanut butter—it's a small thing that I liked. It wasn't going to cause any harm to my health to go without it. It wasn't going to be any great burden to me, but it was going to be a consistent little sacrifice that I could make to God for the intention of the apostolate particularly entrusted to me. And not to overspiritualize, but I really saw a change in the peace and the fruitfulness of the apostolate just by this little sacrifice. Seriously, it worked!

I'd like to offer that idea. If you have somebody in need of prayer—a child who's gone away from the Faith, somebody you need to have a particular conversation with, somebody you're working to forgive, someone you're trying to bring to the Church, whatever it may be—can you be open to God inviting you to make a little sacrifice? Again, this isn't deciding to fast on bread and water or to sleep only four hours a night or to do vigils; it's a little sacrifice. Perhaps it's giving up chocolate chip cookies. Perhaps it's not having alcohol for a period of time or not watching your favorite show.

The specifics of it, such as what you choose to offer and how long you choose to offer it, are up to you. But the idea is simply an intentional, ongoing sacrifice united with prayer for a particular petition.

The second form of uniting prayer with sacrifice, which is my second go-to, is what I call the "life novena." As I'm sure you know, a novena is a nine-day prayer offered for a particular intention or in honor of a particular feast in the Church, and it's very much part of our spiritual tradition. What I do with the life novena is I reflect on what we've already discussed. If we're faithful to Jesus in our daily lives, there's a ton of sacrifices that we're already enduring or already making.

To do a life novena, I say, "OK, for this particular intention, I'm going to offer the next nine days of my life." And I include in that offering all of the sufferings that are usually part of my life. But also, I offer whatever God wants to give me. Of course, this doesn't necessarily mean that something painful is going to happen, but I have this receptivity to whatever God sends. So if I get asked to do a job I don't want to do, I say, "All right, Lord, for the intention of my brother or sister, I'm going to receive this and offer it to you. I'm going to respond to this invitation or this obedience with generosity." Maybe in your house a pipe busts and you have a leak. As part of the life novena, you can say, "All right, Lord, I'm going to fix this leak. I'm going to receive this little burden, this little frustration. I'm not going to lash out. I'm not going to complain. I'm just going to accept this little aspect of my building of the kingdom of God. I'm going to receive this and offer it to you, Lord."

Over and over again, I've seen this practice be incredibly efficacious and fruitful. The life novena is my go-to prayer when an intention is brought to me that deeply moves my heart, whether it is a son or a daughter of somebody I know who has fallen back into addiction, or perhaps it's a family dealing with infertility. Of course, as a friar, particularly as a priest, I'm able to unite each daily sacrifice to the sacrifice of the Mass. But for those of you who don't have access to daily Mass, you can certainly bring these offerings to Sunday Mass and unite them to the offering of Christ in that way.

To summarize, the life novena is the decision to offer the sufferings, the difficulties, and the little irritations of your life for nine days. It's the decision to receive them with a radical surrender and docility to God and his will and providence and to offer them back to him for a particular intention.

QUESTIONS FOR REFLECTION

Is there an intention particularly close to my heart that I just don't know what to do with: a family member who has left the Faith or fallen into addiction, someone struggling in marriage?

Would offering nine days of prayer and sacrifice for this person be something I feel moved to do?

Discerning Sacrifices

Finally, let's just take a look at how to discern making bigger sacrifices. If you're going to make more substantial sacrifices, especially in the area of fasting or some sort of sacrifice of sleep, I encourage you do so with the guidance of somebody you really trust. Ideally, it will be a priest or confessor, a religious, or someone who's been very passionately and deeply and prudently living the spiritual life for many years.

Certainly you have the freedom to make little offerings such as no peanut butter or no chocolate chip cookies, because those aren't going to cause any great harm to your health. And Friday is a great time to continue the practice of abstaining from meat. That's a great thing to do. You do it once a week. It's not going to jeopardize your health necessarily. But if you're going to fast in a bigger way, such as fasting on bread and water, there are a variety of dynamics involved that really do need to be mentored and discerned. Especially for young people, please do not make larger sacrifices without the explicit permission of a confessor, a priest, or a spiritual director, someone very weathered in the spiritual life. Often the spirituality behind the desire to make sacrifices isn't as mature as it needs to be. And then immature or misguided spirituality, especially in the area of sacrifice, can have some long-term negative effects.

We live in a difficult world, and sometimes it's a scary world. We can feel like we're just trying to keep our heads above water. We're just trying to keep our kids from drowning in all the negativity and the mixed messages in the world. We can be tempted to discouragement or despair because we don't feel like we can do anything. We feel like small fish in a big ocean. But let's remember that God is in the business of lifting up the lowly. God is in the business of calling those overlooked or despised by the world to do great things. In particular, he has given us this great dignity, this great power, and this great gift through our Baptism by allowing us to share in his own priesthood. Throughout our lives, we can daily pick up our crosses and follow him, and we can daily cry out and bring to him our needs and our concerns for ourselves, our children, and our loved ones. Let's remember that prayer, united with sacrifice, is powerful. In fact, it is the most powerful force in human history. Like David, we don't fight alone; the Lord of hosts is with us.

As you read this and discern what the next best step might be for you, please know that at 4:45 every morning, a group of struggling but sincere friars are on their knees interceding for the whole world, and this includes you.

CHAPTER SEVEN

Prophets by Baptism: Living a Provocative Life

As a part of our mission here at St. Joseph's Friary in Harlem, the friars regularly go to the streets in search of the homeless and addicted. These encounters help us meet some of the material needs of these people, but most importantly, they give us a chance to befriend them in the name of Christ and his Church.

As a couple of the brothers were visiting our friends on the street, they were told that one of their closest friends, I'll call her Taya, had died on the street. Taya had struggled for years with addiction and fed it through prostitution. She didn't have any family to make sure she received a proper burial, so the friars took it upon themselves to find her body and make sure she had a dignified funeral.

For days, three friars, with nothing more than a first name and description, went from police station to police station trying to find Taya's body and request permission to bury her. Taya didn't carry an ID, and with such limited information the brothers came across dead end after dead end. At the last police station, after the friars shared what they were doing and all of the different places they had looked, the police officer asked with deep interest, "Why are you doing this?" The friar answered, "Because she's our sister, and she deserves it."

I begin with this story because it's what we're going for. We want to live and love in such a way that it provokes questions in our brothers and sisters. Why are you different? What's the reason for your hope? What's the reason for your peace? In other words, we want to live prophetically.

St. John the Baptist lived a radical life in the wilderness. But it was provocative. People would seek him out from all different places to ask him questions. And he would respond by pointing them to the Lamb of God. The authenticity of his life was attractive, so his words were authoritative.

Remember, by our Baptism we are given a share in Christ's functions as Priest, Prophet, and King. While the prophetic call of all the baptized can't be reduced to evangelization, evangelization is a fundamental aspect of it.

An Attractive Life

In this first section, I want to look at making sure our proclamation of the good news of Christ is actually received as good news. There's a moment that is deeply impressed upon my memory: I was at World Youth Day and discerning whether to become a friar. I had just graduated college and was traveling, somewhat providentially, with six friars. I was with them for three weeks. They were amazing friars and great musicians, speakers, and men of prayer and wisdom. But to be honest, I don't really remember a single word that any of them said.

What I do remember is this: At the end of the day, just as the sun was going down, I watched three friars walking to where they were going to stay for the night, laughing and smiling and enjoying each other's company. And just the attractiveness of their friendship and the authentic brotherhood and communion they shared deeply spoke to me. It brought up within me, in a very safe and nonconfrontational way, this desire: "I want that."

And that's what we want our evangelization to do. That's what we want our lives to do. We want this desire to well up in our brothers and sisters: "I want that." There may not be a more provocative or attractive witness we can give the world than through our communion, by being men and women who care about their neighbors and who remain in relationship with their spouses, their families, and their communities. As I've said before, the power of the witness of the Church as family cannot be overestimated.

QUESTIONS FOR REFLECTION

Have I experienced either positive or negative examples of the Church as a family in my parish?

Do I feel that the Church is family and a place where I'm seen, known, and loved? Or do I feel like I'm just a face in the crowd?

Are there ways in my own community or family that I can invite people into the family of God?

Lead with Listening

We want to let our ears speak, to lead with listening. What I'd like to address here is a common strategic error we often fall into, but I'm going to ask you to pay close attention to the distinctions and nuances of this explanation. We're not talking about "Preach the Gospel at all times; if necessary use words." This is not giving you permission to keep your lips sealed. As this 45,000-word book testifies, we believe words are absolutely necessary, but we want to make sure they're effective and are falling upon fertile, receptive soil.

A temptation for many people, often because of fear or insecurity, is approaching evangelization strictly with the attitude that we've got the answer and they don't. To be fair, in a real way that's true. But talking *at* people, giving answers to questions they're not asking, is rarely effective. As a new convert, still in college, I used to tell my buddy that he needed to go to confession. I shot him straight just like that. There was no conversation, no asking him how he was doing. It was just telling him what to do, and guess what, it had probably been more than a decade since his last confession. It didn't work.

Again, words are necessary, but I'd like to invite you to lead with listening. In our work of going after the lost, we want to hear their stories and ask them questions. We want to speak to them prophetically of the dignity of their unique stories, dreams, and fears. After we listen to them and honor them, they'll be much more likely to begin asking us questions and more open to receiving the testimony of our faith. Listening and asking questions is exceptionally effective in tilling the soil of our neighbor's soul and preparing it to receive the seed of the gospel.

Here's what it could look like.

Someone's going to come to us with a question: "Do Catholics worship Mary?" And you could answer on a topical level, but why are they asking that question? What's underneath it? What if you go deep and you ask questions, like "You love the Lord Jesus?" "Yes." "Are you afraid that a relationship with Mary is somehow going to get in the way of giving God the justice and the worship that he's due?" "Yeah, that's what I'm afraid of." If you can ask these questions, then you can say, "No, you know what? We love Jesus too, and we adore Jesus too, and our relationship with Our Lady complements that. It doesn't take away from that."

Jesus said, "As the Father has sent me, even so I send you" (John 20:21). Let's not be afraid to follow the example of Christ, who ate and drank with tax collectors and sinners. I imagine him sitting at the table asking them their stories, their situations, their passions and slowly but surely, through his kind eyes, open ears, and gentle words, drawing them to himself. Let us learn from the Master.

QUESTIONS FOR REFLECTION

Is there anyone in my life who is far from God and who God might be inviting me to reach out to?

When I try to evangelize, do I feel comfortable asking people questions and hearing their stories?

Have I experienced the good news of being listened to in my life?

Provocative Joy

A third dynamic of our prophetic call is that we need to actually be filled with the joy and the hope and the strength of the gospel for our witness to be effective. If we're walking around frowning, angry, cynical, and judgmental of every person or situation we encounter, we're not going to be very attractive witnesses.

We need to actually be filled with the hope, strength, and life of the Holy Spirit. We need to grow in our identity as beloved sons and daughters of the Father and to live from that identity. And intimately linked with this is that we need to be men and women of communion. If we love our brothers and sisters well, as we love those with whom we share our lives well, people will see it and take notice. And that is attractive. That will bring people to us with confidence and trust, because they know we're kind and compassionate. In other words, they may not know how to name it, but they will have seen the fruits of the life of the Holy Spirit within us, just like what I saw in those friars at World Youth Day.

Once others encounter it, they'll want to know more about the roots and the soil from which those fruits were born. In other words, we need to be who we say we are. To be evangelizers, we must first be evangelized. We need to have received the gospel and been transformed little by little by the good news of Christ.

QUESTIONS FOR REFLECTION

In a moment of prayer, can I reflect on the way I've allowed the good news of the gospel to evangelize me first?

Do I experience the hope of Christ's promise and the peace of his presence?

Can I invite the Lord into my heart again, to evangelize me again, so that I may be more effective when sharing the good news with others?

Prophets on Purpose

We want our evangelization and our lives—the prophetic nature of our lives—to be on purpose. So I'll give a brief example. One of my favorite things to do when I'm back home is to get together with some of my buddies and to go play basketball at the gym. When I'm playing, I wear normal basketball clothes, but I wear the Franciscan habit into the gym. Then I change to my basketball clothes, play basketball, have a good time, and talk to the guys.

Even though I'm still pretty sweaty, I put the habit back on before I leave the gym. And by doing that, in a really simple way, I have made all of what I did provocative. I've made it all in the name of Jesus and a public witness to his Church. Often, as I walk in with a habit, play basketball and just bond with friends on the court, and then put the habit back on, guys come with questions—like "So are you a monk or something like that? What do you guys do?" And now there is a really effective space for me to answer questions and to share a little bit of the gospel.

And so, my brothers and sisters, I want to encourage you not to be aggressive but to be *intentional* about evangelization. I want to encourage you to offer a prophetic witness in your places of work, in your homes, and on your teams. When possible, have some public sign of your faith at your work or school, in your car, or around your neck. Have a crucifix or an image of Our Lord or Our Lady, for example, in your office. It's a really fruitful and effective but not confrontational way to let people know that you're a man or woman who is a disciple of Jesus'.

And what this does is, it makes you the religious guy or the religious gal. Of course, if you're not living it faithfully, there are going to be some problems and you're actually going to undermine the witness. But if you are living faithfully, over time you will see results as you build a relationship with others. And when something comes up in the news dealing with faith, or when somebody encounters a difficulty in life and wants to return to God or to the Faith, often they're going to turn to you, the religious one.

And that's important. Again, it's not aggressive. It's not something you can force or make happen. To be effective, it has to happen organically. Simply showing the signs of faith begins to communicate that you're somebody others can talk to about the Faith, which is an important part of marketing. People need to know you've got something to offer before they will come. Of course, as you know, the external sign of your faith is the easy part. To live a deeply provocative and attractive life, the Faith has to actually be real and "in-fleshed" in you.

QUESTIONS FOR REFLECTION

Am I able to recognize a mission field in my life?

Are there people or places where Christ wants me to bring the gospel?

Do I ever make decisions aimed at giving witness to Christ and provoking a conversation? Is there a way I can implement this practice in my life?

Practical Prophets

Let's take a couple of ways in which you can live an attractive prophetic witness.

I remember it as clear as day. When I was a young adult, a few of us went out and played baseball, just having a home-run derby. There were probably ten of us there. One guy was the son of a woman from the church. I didn't have a particular intentionality about evangelization with this guy. I didn't do anything special or out of the ordinary. But his mom told me her son had commented on me. He had said to her, "There was this one kid who wasn't like the other guys. He didn't cuss and he didn't use bad language and he didn't talk about girls in an inappropriate way. What's his story?"

There was something about just the way I spoke, the way I didn't do something evil or wrong, that was noticed by others. And I think that's something that you really want to take note of, on your team, at work, and in your family—how little things go a long way, particularly in the area of the tongue. So we want to make sure that we're not using foul language. As a witness, a prophetic witness to Christ, we also want to avoid gossiping. Imagine if people know, "Yeah, if you want to gossip, don't go to Susan or Brian or John or Beth, because they're not going to add to it and they're actually going to say something nice about the person." This is a deeply provocative witness and a deeply attractive witness.

Another way, which I realize for many people feels unsettling, is doing something as simple as saying a prayer with the Sign of the Cross before you eat your meal, even if it's in public. You can do this as a family. You can do it in your place of work or your school. It's these little signs that show you're a man or woman of faith, that you believe and that it has taken root in the stuff of your life. We have to remember that people want to believe in something. People want to stand for something. People want examples of courage. There's a deep thirsting for authenticity and meaning. And while they may not say anything at first, or they may even make jokes about it, people will notice and be attracted to your freedom to do something in public that could be called controversial. These are ways to till the soil of evangelization by offering a provocative and prophetic witness.

Another little example is abstaining from meat on Friday. While abstaining is not a universal mandate for Catholics around the world, there is something deeply provocative about someone whose faith goes so deep that it affects his or her decisions about what to eat. If you eat with the same people every week, they will know that you don't eat meat on Friday because you're Catholic. There's something beautiful, attractive, and provocative about this witness, and it's not all that difficult to do.

And then finally is this. We need a certain boldness about actually sharing what's going on in our lives. If you went on a retreat over the weekend and someone asks how your weekend was, it's important to share what you did on the weekend and not water it down. If you're going to pray the Rosary with a group at the church one evening during the week, it's important to say so when someone asks, "Oh, what are you doing tonight?" Or if someone asks what you did on the weekend, say, "My family went to Mass on Sunday." You can even share how your family talked about what the priest said.

Essentially, the point is this. If you're reading this book, I know you're living a faithful life and practicing the Catholic Faith. And so you're doing things that other people are not doing. But when you're outside the safe setting of fellow Catholics, there's certainly going to be a temptation to water down the ways you are already practicing the Faith. You will be tempted not to give the full answer when people ask about your activities. But part of living a prophetically attractive life is not hiding it, not putting a bushel basket over it. When someone asks, be willing to share the truth of what you do in a way that is filled with good news.

A little reminder: To be able to answer the question about the "Church thing" you did, you actually have to be doing Church things. We have to be who we say we are.

QUESTIONS FOR REFLECTION

What do I think about these practical proposals?

Are there any ways in which I feel called to give one or two of them a shot?

Effective Evangelization:
Authentic, Articulate, Anointed

We want our evangelization and our building of the kingdom of God to be effective. At the end of the day, it's not just about us clearing our conscience. We actually want our brothers and sisters to enter into relationship with our heavenly Father. We want to spread salvation. We want to grow the family of God. We want to build up the kingdom of God. And so our evangelization needs to be effective. In this final section, we'll break it into three parts. To be effective, our evangelization needs to be authentic, articulate, and anointed.

AUTHENTIC

First of all, you can't give what you don't have. You can't really evangelize if you're not filled with the Holy Spirit and living an authentic life of discipleship. People will see through phoniness, especially people who are with you on a regular basis. And those are the people you have a primary responsibility to introduce to Christ.

So we need to be men and women of prayer and mercy. We need to be men and women who go to confession. When people are brought into our lives, they need to have an authentic experience of discipleship of Christ in the Church. I think the most effective means of evangelization for us as friars is when we bring somebody into our friary. When others share a meal with us or make a holy hour with us, they have this internal experiential encounter, like "Whoa, this is actually real. They actually like each other. They actually pray. They actually live a simple life, and it's incredibly attractive. I feel authentically cared for. I feel authentically listened to."

Over and over, we've had fallen-away Catholics or atheists join us. Because of an authentic encounter with Christ, made experiential through our fraternity, they have come to faith. And that's something beautiful. That's something we want to do as we build friendships— as we build our own kingdom of God in our homes, in our families, and among our friends. If we invite people into it, they can have an authentic, attractive encounter with the living God, the Body of Christ.

This authentic encounter with Christianity well lived is much more effective than an argument is going to be. Therefore, our own discipleship, our family life, and our friendships need to be deeply transformed by the good news of Christ and the transforming power of the Holy Spirit.

ARTICULATE

Second, our faith certainly needs to be articulate. We've talked about giving an attractive and prophetic witness. Part of this witness is to provoke in our brothers and sisters a desire for what we have received and to provoke questions and curiosity. Once those questions have been provoked, we need to be able to speak about what we believe. Well-informed faith is really important. We need to be able to give answers. We need a little background in apologetics so we can explain, for instance, the role of Mary or where the Word of God came from. We need to be able to give a reason for our hope.

And so part of an authentic discipleship is going to be study. We've got to learn—maybe watch some videos or listen to a podcast, find a way to grow in the Faith. As we grow in the truth of Christ, we're going to grow in our capacity and our ability to transmit that truth to our brothers and sisters when they ask questions.

ANOINTED

Finally, for our prophetic witness to be effective and for us to actually make disciples for Jesus Christ, it all has to be anointed. "Unless the LORD builds the house, those who build it labor in vain" (Psalm 127:1). At the end of the day, we are participants in the work of God, and the heavy lifting is the work of God. It is God himself who gives new hearts. It is God himself who gives the gift of faith, and we're just vehicles and instruments.

So we need to pray and ask God's blessing. We want to pray intentionally for the people God has placed in our lives and we feel called to bring to Christ. We need to make sure we're asking for God's help to be authentic men and women of discipleship. We need to ask God's anointing upon our conversations and upon our witness. I'll share one little story of the power of an anointing.

The very first time I ever spoke in public about Jesus I was about eighteen. I was invited to give a brief three-to-five-minute talk to a young-adult group as part of their evening time of prayer with Adoration. And I simply said something along the lines of "We need to take time to listen to God." What I didn't know is that a man had come into the church who had been sort of seeking God. He'd been away from faith for more than twenty-five years. And in his own interior life, God had been saying something to him along the lines of "Stop, slow down, and listen to me."

So when he heard those words come from me, the words were anointed and spoke deeply to this man. They pierced his heart. The next day, Saturday, when I was in line for confession, there was this man in line as well. And he came up to me and said, "You know what? I've been away from confession for more than twenty-five years. But what you said is exactly what God had been saying to me. And so now I'm coming back to the Church." That's the gift of anointing.

We're going to do our part, and we're going to try our best to be faithful. We're going to study and give a real witness and live prophetic lives. But we know that God is in it with us. We know that God has the capacity to turn our very, very little efforts into transformative moments of grace for our brothers and sisters with whom we walk and share our lives and share the dignity of the call to be together in worship of the Father forever.

And so the anointing is a reminder that we need to be men and women of prayer. It's a reminder that we're participants in the grace of the Holy

Spirit but also that the heavy lifting is not up to us. We can have peace, confidence, and freedom to do our best and to share and build up the kingdom with the little portion that has been entrusted to us.

In conclusion, it's the nature of the Church to evangelize. It's the nature of the Church to offer prophetic witness and to share the good news of our Bridegroom and the good news of new life in Christ. We want to share this in a way that is attractive. We want to provoke in our brothers and sisters a spontaneous welling up of desire: "I want that."

We want to live provocative lives, lives that strategically provoke questions so that once the questions have been awakened, we may share the answers with confidence. And we want our prophetic witness to be effective. That means we need to be authentic men and women in our discipleship. We need to be articulate and as well educated in our faith as we can be. And finally, we need to be men and women of prayer, because it's the anointing of the Holy Spirit that makes our efforts fruitful. Apart from him, we can do nothing.

QUESTIONS FOR REFLECTION

Is my evangelization authentic, articulate, and anointed?

Is there a next best step God is inviting me to take in any of these areas?

CHAPTER EIGHT

Kings by Baptism: Cultivating Happiness, Healthiness, and Holiness

I once heard a priest say, "Everybody's got baggage. We're just trying to get it down to a carry-on." That's what this chapter is about: getting your baggage down to a carry-on.

I'd like to begin by quoting from the constitutions of the friars. This quote comes under the section about the virtue of chastity, especially our consecrated chastity, and ways in which we can live that faithfully. After a series of proposals about our prayer, austerity, and fraternal life, this is what our constitution says: The friars are to live out chastity in part by "healthy discipline applied to a balanced way of life made up of prayer, manual labor, study, recreation, and exercise."[10]

Now why are these natural activities proposed as a way to live out the vocation of consecrated chastity, which is a great supernatural vocation? The understanding is that we're human beings and that our humanity and our spirituality are deeply mixed. What affects us on the natural, biological plane is going to have an effect in the spiritual plane.

If you or someone you know has experience with a twelve-step program in dealing with addiction to a substance or an activity, you've probably heard of the acronym HALT. H-A-L-T stands for hungry, angry, lonely, tired. The idea is that if you're experiencing one of these emotions—if you're hungry, angry, lonely, or tired—you're going to be susceptible to self-medicating by acting out in the way you're prone to act out. And so if you are trying to leave sin behind and live a life of great virtue, of radical Christianity and radical generosity, you also have to understand your weakness. You have to understand that if you are not living a balanced life and are consistently hungry, angry, lonely, or tired, you're going to be more susceptible to temptation. You'll be more susceptible to turning to vice to help "balance" things out.

As sharers in the kingship of Christ, we're called to take care of our stuff. We're invited to get our temporal affairs in order and cultivate them so that they are aids in our journey with Christ and not extra baggage that weighs us down.

We're going to look at the way we are called as kings to govern. Before we dive into some of the specifics, let's lay the foundation and make a brief examination of the principle. As Christians, we are baptized into the role of Christ as Priest, Prophet, and King. We've already discussed what it can look like to live as a member of the priesthood of the baptized and to live out our prophetic vocation. So now let's take a look at what it means to be a king. If we go back to the Garden of Eden, we see that God gave Adam a share in his kingship by inviting him to till and keep the Garden, name the animals, and have dominion over them. God has given man a vocation in the world. He's given man a role to play in structuring, organizing, integrating, and cultivating society.

This shouldn't come as a shock. Of course, we have a role to play in organizing our lives—in cultivating a healthy home, a healthy spiritual life, a healthy diet, healthy relationships, healthy rules and regulations, and healthy spaces to communicate. All of these things are going to affect people and our affect our capacity to love one another; therefore, all of these things are also going to affect the way we follow and serve the Lord Jesus. Where there is injustice or irresponsibility or miscommunication, there will be tension, frustration, and often sin and division. An unhealthy life leads to extra baggage. Extra baggage often leads to extra sin.

We're called as kings to cultivate our world and our society. And yes, that does include the political realm and policy making—high-level arenas where the Church really does have a vocation to speak, to help govern and help guide. As salt and light to the world, we as Christians have a responsibility to help govern and help God guide. However, the focus of this chapter is going to be on cultivating a healthy kingdom in *our own lives and families.*

That's because we understand that by living a healthy, well-cultivated, balanced, and integrated life, we're going to thrive as people of happiness, healthiness, and holiness.

The society we live in, particularly the first-world society of the West, is not well integrated or balanced. It does not propose a lifestyle that is conducive to growing in holiness. I can speak to American culture, as I'm familiar with it. A "go-go-go, get-get-get, do-do-do" way of life is proposed and pushed in America in concrete ways in which there are real risks and rewards. But it often means sacrificing a healthy life and healthy relationships.

One clear example is the pressure placed on young people to build up their college applications by being involved in a dozen different activities. And so Mom and Dad have their teenagers always on the go, running from commitment to commitment, creating stress and sometimes leading to burnout. They're always trying to do more instead of living a life of contentment and balance. Why? Because they have to get ahead, because they have to get into the good school. But what's the cost?

Eventually this way of life has a very great cost, because you end up losing your capacity to pray, to be in stillness, and to understand that God is God and God is in control. And growing in your relationship with him is what is most important.

The external stresses weigh on teenagers on a biological level, too. It burdens their relationships. Often they're going to lean toward some sort of entertainment or activity that has the aspect of escapism to help deal with the stress, to self-medicate.

And of course the same can be said of marriages, where there is a great pressure to have things and do things—to acquire achievements, awards, a certain salary, a certain lifestyle. And to get that lifestyle, you have to live a certain way.

But again, what is the cost? There is a cost. We need to take a step back and understand that as Christians, perhaps we are not supposed to be living at the same pace as those who do not know they have a heavenly Father and an everlasting home already prepared for them. This truth invites us to be very intentional in our decisions. It invites us to be very intentional in cultivating our lifestyle and at times in making sacrifices for the greater good of our happiness, health, and holiness.

What we're going to do now is follow the pattern of the proposals that our constitutions make. And we're going to flesh them out for living with a healthy discipline as laity in the world. My brothers and sisters, you have to be the king of your own interior life. In a certain sense, you have to have the autonomy and the capacity to live in freedom and to make decisions according to reason, according to the truth, and not simply according to your passions.

You don't want to be ruled simply by the lower inclinations toward pleasure and comfort. We won't belabor this point too much. But just a reminder that without discipline, there will not be discipleship. Let's be sure to place this act of discipline under the umbrella of kingship. We need to make sure that our intellects and our wills are the kings of our interior life. Why? So that we have the freedom to choose the truth, even though it may be a minority opinion, and to choose the good, even though it may be the difficult or the unpopular choice. So again, my brothers and sisters, discipline is necessary. It requires us to take up our daily cross and follow Christ. Discipline will lead us to freedom. Discipline will lead us to the fullness of relationship with the triune God and is a necessary part of our building the kingdom of heaven.

Let's get rid of the extra baggage.

QUESTIONS FOR REFLECTION

In general, do I feel like I'm living an integrated life?

Am I overworked or overstressed?

Are there external factors I can control that are negatively affecting my relationships, especially my relationship with the Lord?

Made for Motion

Now let's see how we can apply this discipline to manual labor— exercising and using our bodies. We sometimes forget that the daily lives of the first-century Christians were filled with manual labor. And Jesus as a first-century Jewish man lived a life of manual labor and physical exertion. Certainly we see this in his role as essentially a *tekton*, a handyman. Jesus often worked with his hands and his body, and he often must have gone to bed with achy and sore muscles. But also look at what he did with the first disciples. He invited them to follow him and to walk with him. Jesus walked and he walked and he walked. Walking with Jesus required physical exertion. Jesus invited his disciples to hike up a high mountain on a regular basis, and he invited them to take a boat out fishing with him. All of these are activities of great physical exertion. And why is that important? It's important because we have to remember that our bodies are meant to be moved and used. We are made for physical activity, and we are healthiest when we're physically active.

But life in today's world often is not a life of natural physical activity. Certainly there are many jobs in which physical exertion and manual labor are a part of the day-to-day requirements, but more and more men and women are living lifestyles that do not require them to engage in regular physical exertion. But on a biological level, we need it. It's healthy for us. We thrive when we're healthy. And when we're not healthy and when we're not exerting, when we're not seeking wholesome outlets for physical activity, often that's going to have a consequence in our bodies and even in our discipleship.

Many look at physical activity or exercise as going outside for walks or hikes, running on a treadmill, lifting weights, or playing basketball. Whatever kind of exercising you find yourself attracted to, and at whatever level you are safely able to do so, it's important to get in motion.

Also, physical activity is actually an act of discipline. It's a way for us to reclaim, again and again, kingship over ourselves and our interior lives. It's a way for us to do what is difficult when, on a certain level, we may want to just sit on the couch all the time and veg out. Yes, rest is important, but sometimes it's important to push ourselves. We want to grow in the freedom and the capacity to choose the good even when it is difficult.

A beautiful example of this is Fr. Walter Ciszek, a Jesuit priest in the last century who was imprisoned and sent to a Siberian work camp for more than a decade. He was a man of intense virtue, prayer, and strength. And when he was young, he was a man of intense physical activity. He'd often jump in a cold lake and swim to grow in freedom and in the capacity to do what is difficult.

I grew up a country club kid in Orange County, southern California, with a very comfortable life. To this day, in many ways, I'm not the king of my own interior life. I'm not Walter Ciszek. I was never diving in cold lakes so that I could be a free man able to do what is difficult.

So still to this day, as a priest and as a friar, I often find myself struggling with freedom. I often find myself choosing a lesser good because it's an easier good, or I find myself even falling into sin because I lack the freedom to say no and to do what is difficult. One way I can combat this tendency, a way that is remote preparation for these daily battles when temptation comes, is through regular exercise.

Again, extra discipline is necessary for discipleship. And one way we can grow in discipline is through regular physical activity. It's a great form of modern penance and a way to grow in freedom. But it's also really important for us to actually be healthy. We are called to take care of our bodies so we are healthy, to be kings and to govern our bodies. As a king would be responsible for making sure his people are fed and safe and healthy, we have the same responsibility toward our own bodies.

Now, of course, in our society, there's often an idolization of the body or an attitude toward health that is not virtuous. But we as Christians are very capable of making distinctions. I am capable of understanding that I can be healthy and I can exercise because I want to grow in discipleship. I want to be healthy so that I can thrive as a good steward of the body entrusted to me. And I want to be healthy because in the act of being healthy and practicing physical activity, I can strengthen my will and grow in freedom.

QUESTIONS FOR REFLECTION

Is physical activity or manual labor part of my regular routine?

Is there room for growing in this practice?

Am I aware of the way exercising helps to form me in discipline and freedom?

When He Said Rest, He Meant It

On a similar topic, I'd like to talk about sleep. I repeatedly hear young people, especially college students, complaining about sleep. Maybe there is a certain degree to which they are exaggerating it because they feel like it's cool to say, "I only sleep four hours a night." But I think it's true that many people young and old aren't sleeping as well as they should be. Are we always in control of our sleep patterns or our ability to sleep? Of course not, but there might be areas in which we are. In this section, we'll take a look at the factors threatening our rest that we can control.

First of all, people don't sleep because they're too busy. Overextending yourself is a classic form of extra baggage. A remedy, as mentioned before, is developing a disposition of contentment. It is growing in temperance and cutting certain things out of your life. You do this to increase your ability to be healthy, because you want to grow in your freedom and your capacity to respond to the gospel as Jesus is inviting you to do. Prudence is the virtue that helps us say no to good things because they are not coming at the right moment. A well-discerned no coming from a sincere acceptance of our limits is virtuous. Lord, grant us the grace of prudence!

The second big enemy of sleep is our use of TV, entertainment, and social media, especially in the evenings. This is going to affect different generations in different ways, but you may be having difficulty sleeping because you're spending all night scrolling. Perhaps you're only sleeping an hour a night because of that late-night social media binge before you turn out the lights.

My assumption is most people reading this book are not going to be having that difficulty. But if you are, it's good to take a look at it, to ask God's grace, and to sacrificially cut it out. If your eye is causing you to sin, pluck it out. If your social media use or your entertainment use is causing you to lose sleep and hurting you on a biological level, ask God through grace to cut it out.

Of course, many of us lose sleep because of anxiety and stress. From the outset, I'd like to say clearly that not all anxiety is the same. Many people suffer from anxiety for reasons outside their control, and my encouragement for them is to seek the proper professional help: This too is a faithful practice of our "kingship."

The principle audience for the following are those who suffer from anxiety because of the work of their own hands. We're not meant for anxiety.

We'll take a look at two potential causes of anxiety and a foundational remedy. Again, being overextended or overstimulated can be to blame for unnecessary anxiety.

First, as mentioned, we can be overextended in our commitments, and we've already discussed prudently navigating the necessary changes. But we can also be overextended in our expectations. Where these false expectations come from are numerous, but their source is not the most important thing. What's most important is discerning whether the pressures we've put on ourselves for success or social standing are consistent with the gospel. May we find rest in the Lord's expectations for us and experience that his yoke is easy and his burden light.

Second, piggybacking on our conversation about media intake, don't be afraid to cut it out or greatly reduce it in the name of your peace. Again, there are too many factors at play for the scope of this chapter, but be honest with yourself. Is the temptation to compare yourself to others or the sensationalized 24/7 news cycle causing you unnecessary anxiety, stealing your peace, or harming your relationship with the Lord? If so, prayerfully discern cutting back; the extra baggage has got to go.

Finally, a reminder. The deepest remedy for anxiety is being rooted in our identity as beloved sons and daughters of the best of Fathers. It's a medicine we take principally through our times of prayer. Be urgent to cultivate a lifestyle that brings you into this mystery and protects you from the distractions and lies of the enemy.

As we're invited to share in Christ's kingly role, we're also invited to share in his rest. Being unnecessarily tired is not a virtue. We absolutely want to spend all we've got in service of the Lord and his Church. But we lay down our lives in obedience to his invitation, not in obedience to the world. When we lay down our lives in response to the sweet voice of the Good Shepherd, there will be peace and rest in our fatigue. If we do so at the promptings of the world, there will be anxiety in our tiredness and anxiety in our rest. Again, we want to cut out the unnecessary burdens that we're carrying, that weigh us down, hurt our relationships, and leave us vulnerable to temptation. May the Lord give us eyes to see the proper adjustments we should make.

QUESTIONS FOR REFLECTION

Am I overextended in my commitments or expectations?

Is my consumption of media or social media keeping me from peace and Christian rest?

Am I making time to stay rooted in my identity as a beloved child of God?

Food Is Fuel

Let's talk about the "other" heroic moment. As I'm sure many of you have heard, people often talk about the moment your alarm goes off as the heroic moment. It's that first chance of the day to make the hard choice and get out of bed. Of course, it's made harder because you're still sleepy.

A second, less popular heroic moment is the moment you're putting food on your plate. You're hungry, the unhealthy food entices you with its comforts, much like your pillow, and you still have to choose what's best for you. It takes great discipline, but without discipline, there's no discipleship.

Here we want to walk a fine line of not overemphasizing the importance of food but not underestimating it either. The Scriptures implore on our behalf, "May the God of peace himself sanctify you wholly; and may your spirit and soul and body be kept sound and blameless at the coming of our Lord Jesus Christ" (1 Thessalonians 5:23). We're human beings, and we want to be healthy at all levels. Being healthy is a good for its own sake, as it shows proper stewardship of the gift of our bodies, but it also deeply influences our spiritual lives.

Like exercise, healthy eating helps us at a couple of levels. First, it simply helps us function at our highest level. Food is fuel. If we eat well, we'll have the energy we need for the journey. And have no doubt about it: Our capacity to serve others generously and consistently is profoundly linked to our general health and diet.

Second, eating healthily takes great discipline. Properly navigating the temptations of junk food plays a part in our freedom to navigate the rest of the junk the world, the flesh, and the devil bring our way.

QUESTIONS FOR REFLECTION

Do I pay attention to what I eat? Does what I eat fuel me up or slow me down?

Am I aware of the ways my food can strengthen me in following Jesus in other areas of my life?

Recreation That Re-creates

Another recommendation from the friars' constitutions is recreation. For us, this often takes the form of spending time together or developing some "holy hobby." Let's explore this concept by grabbing quotes from different priests.

Fr. Jim Lloyd is an exceptional priest who recently celebrated his ninety-fifth birthday. A regular part of his ministry is accompanying those who struggle with habitual sin, particularly sexual sins. Regularly, he tells the men he walks with, "Make sure you have some good clean fun." Good clean fun gives a moral outlet for our need for enjoyment, friendship, and adventure, which we can also seek through immoral outlets. Intentionally getting together with friends, going hiking, having a nice dinner together, and so forth are very natural ways to stay supernaturally healthy. When we have a full life, we are less prone to fall for the empty promises of temptation.

In a friary, since we don't have TV or internet, we need one another for these times of recreation. Most Sundays will find brothers playing basketball together, going on a hike, playing a board game, having a jam session, or enjoying some other form of good clean fun. It's healthy and helpful for holiness.

I was also struck by a senior priest who shared that he always tells couples in marriage prep to make good memories together. The idea is to go on trips or adventures together to make sure you have a memory bank full of smiles and laughs so that when difficult times come, you can cash those memories in.

Difficulties in our relationships are going to make us susceptible to sin. While creating good memories together isn't going to eradicate all relationship struggles, it can certainly be a help. My encouragement for you with your community—your spouse, family, or friends—is to create some good times together. We're made for intimacy. If we don't find it within our family, friends, and faith, we'll try to find it another way.

The common thread from both of these recreation proposals is that they are done in relationship and not isolation. Remember, the friars are hard-core Jesus followers. And as men striving to give everything to Jesus, we prioritize communal recreation because it's a support and not a stumbling block to our laying down our lives for Christ and his Bride, the Church.

QUESTIONS FOR REFLECTION

Do I have "holy" hobbies and forms of recreation?

Am I regularly working good clean fun into my life?

Do I prioritize spending time with my family and friends?

The Altar of the Desk

"The altar of the desk" is what they called studying during seminary. They called it this because they knew studying was a sacrifice. Studying is difficult. It requires patience and discipline. It's also important.

I won't belabor the point, especially because I'm probably preaching to the choir. You wouldn't have made it so far into this book if you didn't value learning about your faith and ways to put it into practice. My encouragement is to continue with this practice. It forms the mind while strengthening the will.

I'd also like to encourage your studying in other areas you find interesting: history, geography, music, or other fields. All of these studies of the good things of creation can lead us back to the good Creator.

Study, or what I imagine as fruits and vegetables for the mind, fills you up so you have less of an appetite for the junk food of empty entertainment and dessert-esque distractions.

QUESTIONS FOR REFLECTION

Am I reading books or learning something new that is life-giving?

Is there a topic I haven't studied but I'm interested in that I could begin exploring?

We've been given a job to do and the tools to do it. Let's not be afraid of our humanity or ignorant of it. We're making a profoundly spiritual journey in an authentically human way. The human stuff matters. Through healthy living—a prudent governing of our personal lives—we'll set ourselves up for success in growing in happiness and holiness. While we know Jesus can handle our extra baggage, he also doesn't want us to carry more than is necessary. May he help us get it down to a carry-on.

CHAPTER NINE

Renewal That Lasts: The Mechanics of Conversion

If you've ever been in the habit of making a regular confession, you probably have a memory like this. You make a good examination of conscience and a sincere confession, and you are totally committed to not falling back in the same sins again. Maybe a couple of hours or days or weeks or maybe even a month goes by, and then you look at your life and realize you've fallen back into the same sins you really thought you were going to leave behind. It's a situation that I have encountered again and again, both as a penitent and as a confessor. I go to confession or I receive a penitent, and I'm totally sincere or they're totally sincere and committed to changing. But after a little bit of time, we find ourselves back where we started.

After reflecting on this over the years, I've come to a hypothesis. I propose that the reason we're not really having radical conversions and not really leaving sin behind is not a matter of sincerity but one of strategy. To help explain what I mean, I'd like to take a look at the stuff of long-term behavior change, the mechanics of conversion, in light of a pithy little phrase:

If nothing changes, nothing changes.

You see, the change of leaving sin behind and adopting a new behavior is actually going to be the fruit of changes at a much deeper level of our humanity and lived experience. The change in behavior is going to be the fruit of a change at the level of our intellect, our will, our emotions or passions, our environment or context, or some mixture of all these. We'll have a chance in this chapter to focus on each of these areas in a little bit more detail, but first I'd like to share an introduction.

A Bird's-Eye View

What sorts of changes lead to behavior change? At the level of the intellect, behavior change happens when we acquire a new truth or let go of a previously held lie. At the level of the will, which is like the decision-making muscle, it happens as we strengthen or weaken the will. At the level of the emotions or passions, which can change very, very frequently, we often experience conflicting or contradictory desires or movements; as our feelings ebb and flow, they push us to make decisions based on what we are feeling most strongly at a given moment. Finally, at the level of our context or our environment, behavior change happens when a new person or a new factor or reality comes into our situation.

So the hypothesis is that we don't have the long-term behavior change we want because we're not actually going deep enough when we try to bring a solution to the problem. So let's look at the deeper levels of change that can bring about much deeper conversion and longer-lasting results.

The Renewal of Your Mind

In Romans, St. Paul reminds us, "Do not be conformed to this world but be transformed by the renewal of your mind" so that you may judge "what is good and acceptable and perfect" (Romans 12:2). In other words, St. Paul is telling us to have a renewal—have a change—at the level of our intellect so that we may have a radical change in the orientation of our entire life. And St. Paul is a perfect example. While St. Paul, called Saul at the time, was on his way to Damascus to persecute Christians, he got knocked to the ground and heard the voice of Jesus say, "Saul, Saul, why do you persecute me?" Saul replied, "Who are you?" And he heard the voice of Jesus say, "I am Jesus." (See Acts 9:1-5.)

We all know what happened: Saul had a radical life change. He became known as Paul, and instead of persecuting Christians, he started to make Christians. And what was the radical change that happened in his life? He realized that Jesus was the Messiah, and this truth transformed his life.

Now, let's bring it down to our level and see how this transformation works in our everyday life. We see it, for example, in a young woman who realizes with joy that she's now pregnant. There's a new truth. She now knows that she's pregnant, and so what happens? She starts making a series of changes and takes action. She makes appointments for the doctor. She may quit smoking or drinking. Right? It's a simple pattern: A new truth is revealed, and therefore what follows will be a new series of actions.

Another example is a rock-bottom moment. When someone hits rock bottom, he has a moment to see that if something doesn't radically change, he's going to lose everything. Often it's the experience of this truth that catapults an addict toward a life of sobriety. Where there is a new truth, there is going to be a new way of life. In many ways, we know that the greatest conversions we need to have are going to be the fruit of the renewal of our minds coming more and more into contact with the fullness of the truth revealed to us in Jesus Christ.

If we go back to that experience of going to confession, we can see this. At the moment of confession, each of us is very aware of our guilt or distaste for sin. We're experiencing it acutely, and this is emphasized as we reveal it to the priest. And we know we don't want to do it again. But what happens as time goes on is that truth, which at the moment of confession is at the forefront of one's mind, slowly but surely fades to the background and becomes a less important and less potent memory. And so, when temptation comes again or a difficulty comes again, we slide back very easily toward that sinful behavior without ever rubbing up against this truth that we once experienced so poignantly—the truth that we don't want to do that again. It doesn't make us happy. It leaves us sad, guilty, and remorseful.

It's just the way our minds work. We need reminders and direction, and we need to very intentionally focus on what we're trying to do. If we don't have a direction, we're going to get lost. My proposal is to focus on one, two, or three areas in your life where you really want to grow: one, two, or three sins that you really want to leave behind or virtues that you really want to strengthen and develop. Write them down. Share them with a friend. Share them with someone who's walking on this journey with you. And every day in prayer, ask for God's grace to be faithful to these commitments.

Ask for God's grace to be convicted of these truths, and then follow up. In the middle of the day, take a moment to pray. I'd suggest implementing the three-by-five examen laid out in the chapter on prayer. And then in the evening, call to mind these one, two, or three areas. See how you did. If there was a fault, ask God's mercy. If there was a success, give him praise and ask for his help to do better again the next day. What we're trying to do through Christian memory and intentional living is fight this human tendency to forget who we are, where we're going, and what we're all about. And as we continue this journey little by little and continue to pray, we can be renewed more and more, like St. Paul. As we continue to fill our lives with the light of Christ and keep out the darkness of sin, we too can be transformed by Christ into the saints we're called to be.

Work the Will, but Don't Overestimate It

Now let's take a look at the will. The will, as mentioned before, is the decision-making muscle. It's the power of the soul that chooses. We want our will to be strong so that we can choose the good when it's difficult and avoid evil when it's pleasurable.

The analogy of a muscle is going to be really important to us in this section because first, like a muscle, the will can grow stronger as it's exercised. But like a muscle, if the will is not exercised, it's going to atrophy and grow weaker. And second, like a muscle, the will is ordinarily going to grow and get stronger incrementally or decline incrementally. It's not typical to see huge changes in our willpower overnight, but we can have huge changes in our willpower over a journey. In some ways, we've already started to address the ways to care for our will in the section on balanced living. It's good to remember that if we're tired, if we're lonely, if we're stressed, if we're not exercising, or if we're eating too much sugar, these things are going to have an effect on our will. They are going to make us vulnerable to sin.

Now let's take a really close look at the mechanics of the will in the area of our confession and firm amendment to change and the unfortunate but frequent lack of change. When we go to confession, we tend to be acutely aware of what we're trying to do and where we're trying to go, and that is extremely helpful. But when we go to confession, we also often experience a distaste for our sinful behavior at the level of our emotions or our desires. The sin is unattractive, even repulsive to us. So the felt experience is "I know where I want to go. And I know where I don't want to go, and I am repulsed by the thought of going back there." We feel like we're very well set up for success.

But this can lead us to a false sense of security. If we're not deeply committed to remembering and we're not deeply committed to taking care of our environment or our context, what often happens is that we just assume we're going to be strong enough in the future to do better. Our assumption is based on what we're experiencing at the moment of confession. We're not feeling the pinch. It's easy to feel like we're going to choose the good and avoid the evil when the good feels good and the evil feels evil. And so we often go back to living just as we used to live before. There is no change, and so there are no changes.

We're betting on having a big change in our willpower, but as I said, the will, like a muscle, grows and strengthens very slowly and over time. When life happens and we're less aware of why we're trying to live differently, or when our desires do a 180 and now are attracted to and hungering for what was repulsive at the moment of confession, we fall back into the same behavior. Why? Because in fact we're not strong enough to hold back our disordered passions at that moment. We fall again.

The changes we need to make immediately need to compensate for the fact that the changes at the level of the will are going to take place gradually. In other words, if your strategy is "I'm just going to do better next time," your strategy needs to change.

Throughout the book, we've shared a variety of ways to work the will-muscle: exercise, healthy eating, study, refraining from gossip, and so on. We certainly want to work the will every day, but we also want to have realistic expectations about the pace at which it grows.

What Do You Really Want?

So let's take a look at the emotions and the passions. Our passions, desires, emotions, and hungers change often, sometimes very quickly and dramatically. A good Christian anthropology understands that our passions need to be guided by our intellect and our will, by truth and by freedom. If they're not, we're going to fall into a type of slavery to the whims of our passions. Passions can be strong forces for decision, but they are terrible at perceiving and pursuing objective truth.

A popular image is that the passions are like horses attached to a chariot. The horses pulling the chariot need to be directed and held firm by the charioteer and the reins. If they're properly ordered, they can drive us toward a great love and a great life. If they're disordered, they're going to go all over the place and lead us to disaster. It can be felt as unfortunate, but it's true that we don't have a ton of control over our emotions. We're not impotent before them, but we're not omnipotent before them either. So we want to have a great strategy in place for changes at the level of the intellect and the will and the environment so that we can navigate well the changes that are prone to happen at the level of the emotions or passions.

Sticking with the theme of this chapter, I'm going to propose one takeaway for you. I'd like you to pay attention to the different levels of your desires. For example, perhaps you have a desire on a deep level to be healthy. You want to eat well. You want to have energy. But also, on another level, you really want to sit on the couch eating cookies and chips. And so we feel this tension. Depending on a variety of factors, including force of habit, we're either going to choose the chips and couch and cookies more often and then feel some sort of sadness afterward, or we're going to choose to exercise and eat clean and enjoy the fruits of a happy, healthy life.

The same thing happens in moral issues. We might feel a desire to be a man or woman of heroic virtue and heroic love. We may want to be a great disciple and a great father or mother, son or daughter, sister or brother. But also we're going to experience a desire for sinfulness and self-protection—pettiness, gossip, lust, and so on. If we choose those things, there's going to be a passing pleasure that leads to a prolonged disappointment and sadness. But if we choose the good again and again, there's going to be joy. There's going to be freedom. There's going to be contentment. And it will be contagious.

So what I'd like you to do now and on occasion in the future in your time of prayer and self-reflection is call to mind these questions:

Who do I really want to be? What do I really desire in my life? Is comfort going to control me, or is the invitation of Christ to greatness going to control me?

If we can intentionally and consistently call to mind our deepest desires as those passing temptations toward sinful pleasures come and go, we'll be firmly rooted. And as we grow in the habit of choosing the narrow road, the road less traveled, the road of sanctity, the easier it will be.

An Environment That Evangelizes

Let's take a look at creating what we could call an environment that evangelizes, or a context that sets us up for success. Again, I'd like to give a natural example. If you're cruising down the freeway in your car and then you look up ahead and see a police officer on the side of the road, what are you going to do? Most likely, the first thing you're going to do is take your foot off the gas pedal and look down at your speedometer to make sure you're not speeding. There's a new person in your environment, the police officer, and the fruit of that is going to be a change in behavior. There's a change in your behavior because there's a change in your context.

You may have had this experience as a young man or woman when your crush came in the room. As he or she enters, maybe you start standing a different way, talking a different way, flipping your hair a different way, joking a different way to make a good impression or to get his or her attention. In other words, another person entered your context, your environment, and because of that, you changed your behavior. It's something we experience every day. It's something we actually talk about in Christianity more often in the negative, using the term "the occasion of sin." What we mean by the occasion of sin is a situation or a context that is often going to result in our choosing a sinful behavior. For a struggling alcoholic, this could be going to a party or a bar. For a young unmarried couple, this could be spending time in a house or an apartment alone together, particularly in the evening. These are moments or situations that often lead to bad choices.

Certainly, as part of setting ourselves up for success and having a change in context, one of the first changes we want to make with urgency is keeping ourselves out of occasions of sin. In many ways, this is the low-hanging fruit, because we're able to make these decisions before our passions are awakened or fed with a particular desire in a negative situation. For example, it's much easier not to enter a tempting situation with your boyfriend or girlfriend than it is to choose chastity once you're together and alone. Similarly, it's much easier not to go grab another beer or cookie or donut if you don't keep them in your pantry. If you keep them away, you're much less likely to make the trip to the store to buy whatever it is you're trying to avoid, because your passions, desires, and appetites are protected by your environment.

Many of us know that pornography is a plague that afflicts countless men and women, and one of the reasons we don't leave it behind is not because we don't want to but because we so consistently put ourselves in occasions of sin. For those who have had a past or current struggle with pornography, having your computer or smartphone in a place where there is internet and privacy is often an occasion of sin. Perhaps being in that situation doesn't lead you to fall into sin immediately. Maybe it takes a few hours. Maybe it takes a few days or weeks. But slowly and surely, the appetite grows and the firm amendment of resolve weakens and the reason you're trying to avoid the sin gets hazier. And so you choose to sin again and fall back into this sin. Each fall feeds and grows the appetite, weakens the will, and makes it hard to say no in the future.

So instead of trying to be heroic in the difficult moment, let's simply be smart. Let's take a look at our lives, our environments, our contexts, and root out anything that is going to be an occasion of sin. Place things that could be an occasion of sin in environments that are healthy and safe and secure. You're much less likely to fall into pornography if your computer or smartphone is always left in a public place. Those who have access to these things in privacy sincerely don't want to sin, but their strategy is broken. If nothing changes, nothing changes.

Now let's take a look at the positive changes we can make in our environments. There can perhaps be nothing better for setting yourself up for success than sharing your journey with another. Make a positive change by inviting at least one other person into your life to walk with you. This can be a spouse or a confessor or a friend you trust. If you know you're going to share what you're doing with another, in some ways, you're never totally alone. It's the power of an accountability partner or a sponsor, as we see in AA. My brothers and sisters, Jesus sent the disciples out in twos, and this is no accident. We're not meant to make this journey alone.

There's a famous line from St. Irenaeus that the glory of God is man fully alive.[11] The man who lives as an island is not the man fully alive and therefore not the glory of God. Man in communion is man fully alive, the glory of God. We need one another. The world is enriched and attracted by our communal journey. Don't try this alone.

You Are Called to Radical Discipleship

If you have picked up this book and made it this far, there's no doubt you're as sincere as can be. You want to live radical discipleship in the midst of a crazy world. My great fear or sadness is that you may read this book, be inspired, make decisions to change, but then end up back in the same place as weeks, months, and years go by.

That's not to say you can't start again if you backslide. Jesus is very clear about this in his parables. Just know that this book is meant to be a source of conversion, of authentic, deep, and permanent renewal in your life through the grace of the Holy Spirit. My brothers and sisters, as you seek to apply these new commitments and new truths and new ideas, do it sincerely and do it strategically. Focus on the area where you feel the Lord calling you to grow. What is it specifically? Keep before your eyes who you are and where you're going.

Remember, do not overestimate the strength of your will. Protect the muscle as it grows. Exercise it, but protect it. Protect it particularly by not placing yourself in occasions of sin. Protect it too by seeking the support of your brothers and sisters, by sharing your journey and your burden with them. We seek to keep our emotions and our passions guided by our intellects and our wills, so that we may be truly free. But let's also pay attention to who we really want to be. Let's pay attention to that deep desire planted in our hearts to be men and women of renewal in this world. Pay attention to that desire to participate in God's bringing cosmos and order and peace out of chaos and disorder and tension. Let's beg the Holy Spirit for the grace to be who we say we are with all sincerity of heart and all strategy of mind. May we make changes so that we may be truly changed and be instruments of change and renewal and rebuilding in the Church and the world, which we see so often falling into ruins.

I'd like to close by offering to you words St. Francis addressed to his brothers as he prepared for his passing from this life to the next: "Let us begin, Brethren, to serve our Lord God, for until now we have made but little progress."[12] "I have done what was mine to do, may Christ teach you what is yours."[13]

In you, Lord, is our hope, and we shall never hope in vain.

May St. Francis, St. Clare, and all of the seraphic saints intercede for you and your loved ones.

CLOSING DEDICATION

Hail, Our Lady of Guadalupe, my mother and queen. I, your little son, dedicate this work to you and entrust its fruitfulness to your prayers. May all who read it experience your maternal care and be enkindled with a seraphic love for your beloved son, our Lord, Jesus Christ.

Salutation of the Blessed Virgin Mary

Hail, Lady, Holy Queen,
Holy Mother of God, Mary!
You who are virgin made Church and
chosen by the most heavenly Father!
You whom he consecrated with his most holy
beloved Son and the Holy Spirit, the Paraclete!
You in whom there was and is total fullness
of grace and every good!
Hail his palace, hail his tabernacle, hail his home!
Hail his vestment, hail his handmaid, hail his mother!
And hail all of you, holy virtues,
which, by the grace and illumination of the Holy Spirit,
are poured into the hearts of the faithful to
make the faithless faithful to God.

— **St. Francis of Assisi** (translated by Fr. Solanus Benfatti, CFR)

APPENDIX

Contentment Check for the Laity

Based on the poverty check of the Franciscan Friars of the Renewal.

A discernment tool recommended for use four times a year:
January 1, April 1, July 1, October 1

What has inspired my understanding of Christian simplicity lately (a Scripture, other reading, encounter with the poor, etc.)?

How is it that Christ's own poverty is kept before me and informs my life?

Have I been in contact with Christ in the distressing disguise of the poor?

How can I grow in a spirit of humility and poverty of spirit and imitate the Heart of Christ?

Am I growing in trust of our heavenly Father and his providential care for me?

Do I carry myself with a spirit of gratitude for the things I do have?

Do I have a spirit of holy detachment from the goods of this earth? What do I cling to and why?

Am I able to find meaning in simpler things?

How much time, energy, and worry do I dedicate to purchasing material possessions?

Have I been distracted by internet "window shopping?"

Do I purchase things because I need to or because I like the feeling of getting something new for its own sake?

Am I burdened by a need for more accumulation of goods?

Have I felt any freedom in living in a simpler way?

Have I cultivated a spirit of contentment? Am I able to say "That's enough" to the latest ad or item I like?

Can I think of a time I said no to a purchase because of a desire to live more simply? How did that feel?

Have I created and kept to a budget with myself or my family, ensuring that a portion is set aside for the poor?

Do I actively look for ways to live more simply so that I can better provide for those in need?

Do I have any items in my possession that are unnecessary and could be given to another in greater need? Are there three things I own that I can give away?

Have I made any purchases unnecessarily? How can I resolve to do better in the future?

Have I been wasteful with food or spent money unnecessarily?

Are there any practical ways I can store up treasure in heaven—works of charity, almsgiving, etc.?

How has living more simply affected my relationship with Christ?

Has living more simply given me any new insight into Christ's own poverty?

NOTES

1   Prayer of St. John Paul II at La Verna on September 17, 1993, quoted in Michael A. Perry, "Homily of the Minister General for the Feast of the Stigmata of St. Francis of Assisi," *OFM* (blog), September 17, 2020, ofm.org.

2   The three-by-five examen is inspired by a conversation I had with a Jesuit, who told me he had learned about it in his formation.

3   This popular quote is paraphrased from Fyodor Dostoyevsky, *The Idiot* 3.5.

4   Frank Sheed, *Theology and Sanity* (1946; repr., San Francisco: Ignatius, 1993), 22.

5   For example, see "Links Between Childhood Religious Upbringing and Current Religious Identity," Pew Research Center, October 26, 2016, pewforum.org.

6   Franciscan Friars of the Renewal, *Constitutions and Directory* (2016), C56.

7   Franciscan Friars of the Renewal, C14.

8   "Our History," Mary's Meals, accessed October 19, 2020, marysmeals.org.

9   Extract from a sermon by Leo the Great, from the Office of Readings for Christmas, *The Liturgy of the Hours*, vol. 1, trans. International Commission on English in the Liturgy (New York: Catholic Book Publishing, 1975), 404.

10 Franciscan Friars of the Renewal, *Constitutions and Directory*, D21.1.

11 See Irenaeus, *Against Heresies* 4.20.6–7.

12 Francis, quoted in Bonaventure, *The Life of Saint Francis*, trans. E. Gurney Salter (London: Dent, 1904), 14.1.

13 Bonaventure, 14.3.

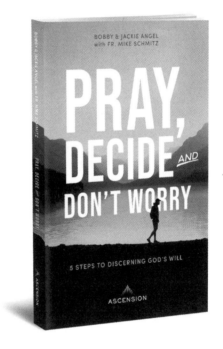

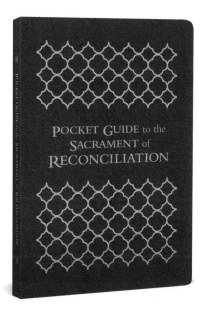